W9-ACL-929

GLOBETROTTER™
Travel Atlas

SOUTH AFRICA

NEW
HOLLAND

New Holland Publishers (UK) Ltd
London • Cape Town • Sydney • Auckland

First edition	1994
Second impression	1995
Third impression	1996
Fourth impression	1997
Second edition	1997
Second impression	1998
Third impression	2000
Third edition	2001
Fourth edition	2003
Fifth edition	2005
Sixth edition	2006
Seventh edition	2009
Eighth edition	2010

10 9 8 7 6 5 4 3 2 1

website: www.newhollandpublishers.com

Garfield House, 86 Edgware Road
London W2 2EA
United Kingdom

80 McKenzie Street
Cape Town 8001
South Africa

Unit 1, 66 Gibbes Street
Chatswood NSW 2067
Australia

218 Lake Road
Northcote, Auckland
New Zealand

Distributed in the USA by
The Globe Pequot Press, Connecticut

ISBN 978 1 84773 833 2

Publishing Manager: Thea Grobbelaar
DTP Cartographic Manager: Genené Hart
Editors: Thea Grobbelaar, Carla Redelinghuys, Alicha van
Reenen, Melany Porter, Tarryn Berry
Designer: Nicole Bannister
Cartographers: Nicole Bannister, Genené Hart
Compiler/Verifier: Denielle Lategan, Elaine Fick
Reproduction by Hirt & Carter, Cape Town
Printed and bound by Times Offset (M) Sdn. Bhd., Malaysia.

Cover: *Quiver tree and wild flowers, Goegap Nature Reserve.*
Title Page: *The Wilderness coastline, part of the well-known
Garden Route.*

Photographic Credits:
Herman Potgieter, page 33; IOA/Shaen Adey,
pages 49, 59; IOA/CLB, page 24; IOA/Roger de la
Harpe, pages 30, 67; IOA/Gerhard Dreyer, title
page, page 40; IOA/Walter Knirr, pages 10, 16,
18, 54, 70 (bottom), 72, 80; IOA/Peter Pickford,
page 74; IOA/Erhardt Thiel, pages 46, 48, 50;
IOA/Hein von Hörsten, cover, pages 35, 39, 62;
IOA/Lanz von Hörsten, pages 20, 42, 45, 78;
IOA/Keith Young, pages 26, 28, 57, 61, 70 (top).
[IOA: Images of Africa; CLB: Colour Library]

This atlas has been written by independent authors
and updaters. The information therein represents their
impartial opinion, and neither they nor the publishers
accept payment in return for including in the book or
writing more favourable reviews of any of the estab-
lishments. Whilst every effort has been made to
ensure that this guidebook is as accurate and up to
date as possible, please be aware that the facts quot-
ed are subject to change, particularly the price of
food, transport and accommodation. The Publisher
accepts no responsibility or liability for any loss, injury
or inconvenience incurred by readers or travellers
using this atlas.

**Emergency Telephone Numbers
Notrufnummern
Appels d'Urgence**

Police
Polizeirevier   10111
Poste de police

Telephone enquiries
Telefonauskunft   1023
Information téléphonique

Ambulance
Krankenwagen   10177
Ambulances

Below: *This brightly coloured South African flag was
first raised at midnight on 26 April 1994. For most South
Africans it is a symbol of hope, uniting the nation in its
effort to reconciliate and become a truly democratic
society.*

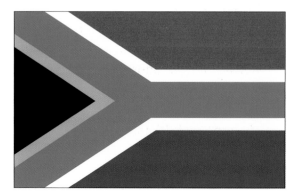

CONTENTS

TOURIST AREAS

MAIN MAP SECTION

INDEX

For ease of use, the Index has been divided into two sections:

• the first focuses on the Tourist Area Maps and related text and photographs.

• the second deals with the Main Map Section only, facilitating the easy location of cities, towns and villages.

National Route Planner

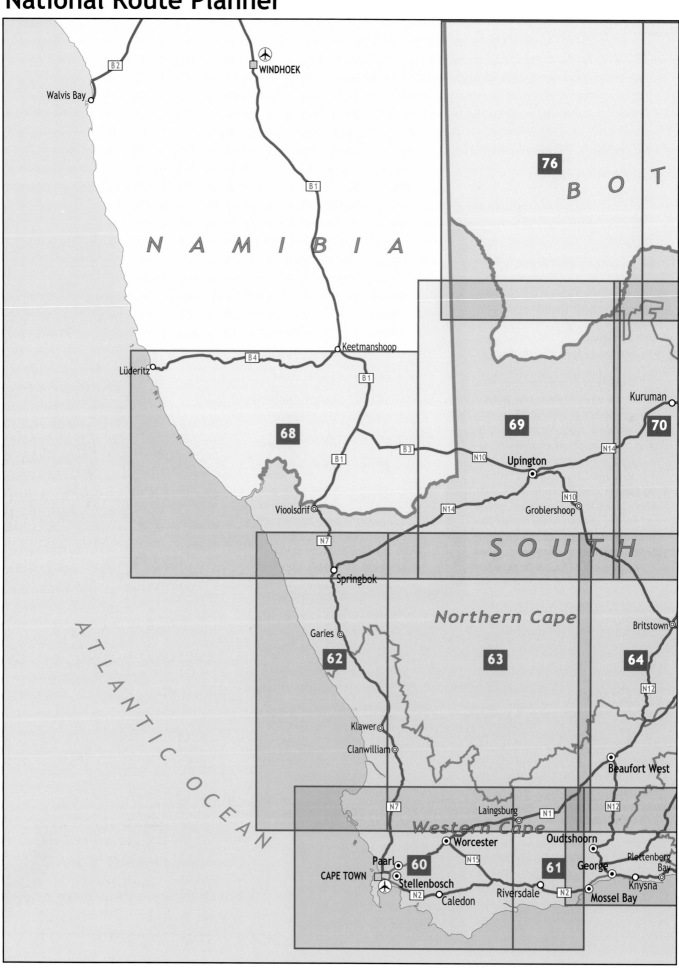

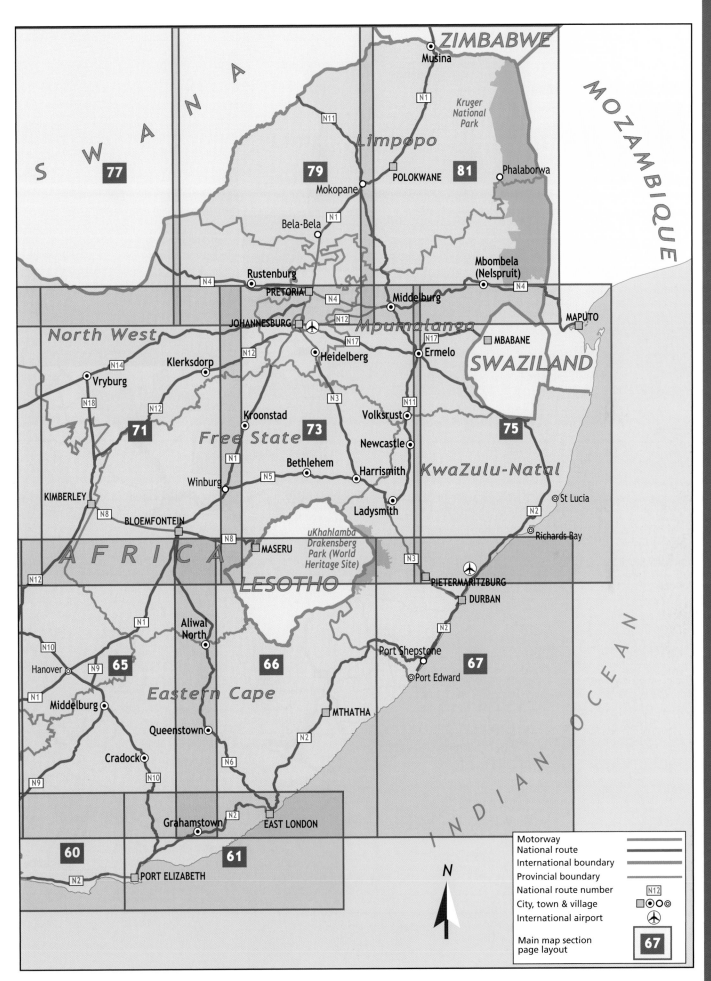

Tourist Area Planner

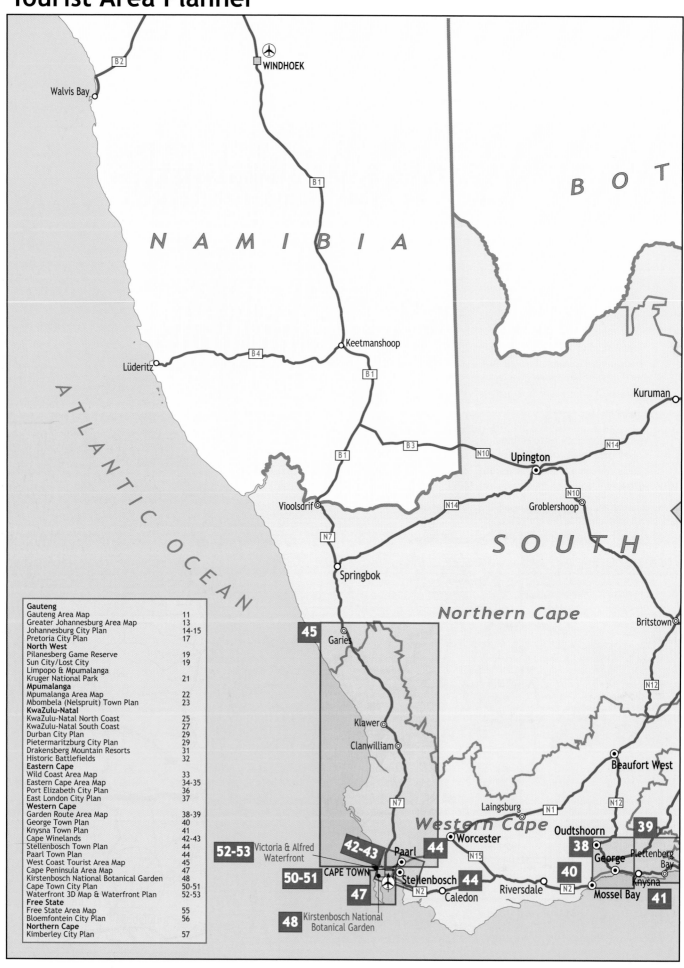

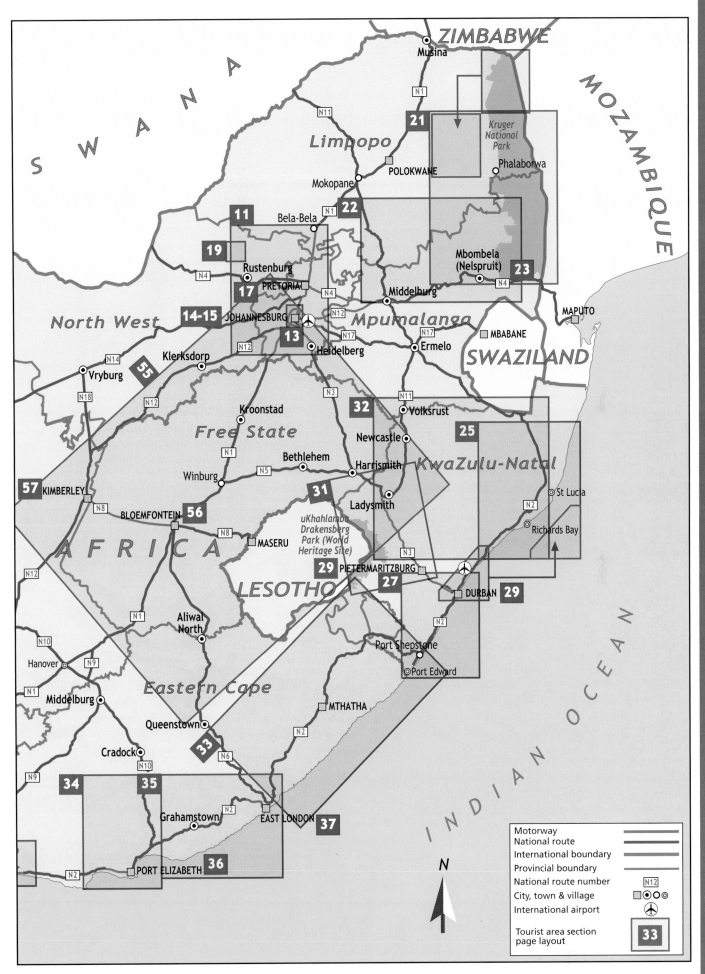

Distance Chart

APPROXIMATE DISTANCES IN KILOMETRES	BLOEMFONTEIN	CAPE TOWN	DURBAN	EAST LONDON	GABORONE	GRAHAMSTOWN	JOHANNESBURG	KIMBERLEY	MAPUTO	MASERU	MBABANE	PORT ELIZABETH	PRETORIA	WELKOM	WINDHOEK
BEAUFORT WEST	544	460	1178	605	1042	492	942	504	1349	609	1129	501	1000	697	1629
BLOEMFONTEIN		1004	634	584	622	601	398	177	897	157	677	677	456	153	1593
BRITSTOWN	398	710	1032	609	791	496	725	253	1289	555	1075	572	783	551	1378
CAPE TOWN	1004		1753	1099	1501	899	1402	962	1900	1160	1680	769	1460	1156	1500
COLESBERG	226	778	860	488	848	375	624	292	1123	383	903	451	682	379	1573
DE AAR	346	762	980	557	843	444	744	305	1243	503	1023	520	802	499	1430
DURBAN	634	1753		674	979	854	578	811	625	590	562	984	646	564	2227
EAST LONDON	584	1079	674		1206	180	982	780	1301	630	1238	310	1040	737	1987
GABORONE	622	1501	979	1206		1223	358	538	957	702	719	1299	350	479	1735
GEORGE	773	438	1319	645	1361	465	1171	762	1670	913	1450	335	1229	926	1887
GRAAFF-REINET	424	787	942	395	1012	282	822	490	1321	599	1101	291	880	577	1697
GRAHAMSTOWN	601	899	854	180	1223		999	667	1478	692	1418	130	1057	754	1856
HARRISMITH	328	1331	306	822	673	929	282	505	649	284	468	1068	332	258	1921
JOHANNESBURG	398	1402	578	982	358	999		472	599	438	361	1075	58	258	1801
KEETMANSHOOP	1088	995	1722	1482	1230	1351	1296	911	1895	1245	1657	1445	1354	1205	505
KIMBERLEY	177	962	811	780	538	667	472		1071	334	833	743	530	294	1416
KLERKSDORP	288	1271	645	872	334	889	164	308	763	368	525	1009	222	145	1693
KROONSTAD	211	1214	537	795	442	812	187	339	742	247	522	888	245	71	1724
LADYSMITH	410	1413	236	752	755	932	356	587	567	366	386	1062	422	340	2008
MAFIKENG	464	1343	821	1048	158	1065	287	380	886	544	648	1141	294	321	1577
MAPUTO	897	1900	625	1301	957	1478	599	1071		853	223	1609	583	813	2400
MASERU	157	1160	590	630	702	692	438	334	853		633	822	488	249	1750
MBABANE	677	1680	562	1238	719	1418	361	833	223	633		1548	372	451	2162
MBOMBELA (NELSPRUIT)	757	1762	707	1226	672	1358	355	827	244	616	173	1434	322	639	2156
MTHATHA	570	1314	439	235	1192	415	869	747	1064	713	1003	545	928	718	2066
MUSINA	928	1932	1118	1512	696	1529	530	1002	725	960	808	1605	472	788	2331
OUDTSHOORN	743	506	1294	704	1241	532	1141	703	1705	959	1417	394	1199	896	1828
PIETERMARITZBURG	555	1674	79	595	900	775	509	732	706	511	640	905	567	485	2148
POLOKWANE	717	1721	907	1301	485	1318	319	791	605	749	515	1394	261	577	2120
PORT ELIZABETH	677	769	984	310	1299	130	1075	743	1609	822	1548		1133	830	1950
PRETORIA	456	1460	646	1040	350	1057	58	530	583	488	372	1133		316	1859
QUEENSTOWN	377	1069	676	207	999	269	775	554	1302	423	1240	399	833	525	1829
UPINGTON	588	894	1222	982	730	851	796	411	1395	745	1157	945	854	669	1005
WELKOM	153	1156	564	737	479	754	258	294	813	249	451	830	316		1679
WINDHOEK	1593	1500	2227	1987	1735	1856	1801	1416	2400	1750	2162	1950	1859	1679	

Strip Route

Strip Routes

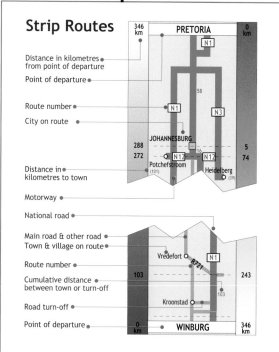

Distance in kilometres from point of departure

Point of departure

Route number

City on route

Distance in kilometres to town

Motorway

National road

Main road & other road
Town & village on route

Route number

Cumulative distance between town or turn-off

Road turn-off

Point of departure

Strip Routes

Strip routes are located throughout the atlas to indicate the distances between major centres in a specific region. Distances between other towns and villages along the route are also shown.

Distance Charts

In order to calculate the distance between two of the country's major centres, locate the name of the first town or city on the vertical or horizontal column on the chart (see above), then locate the name of the other on the second column and read off the number where the vertical and horizontal columns intersect.

Toll Road Chart

Various South African provinces are served by time-saving toll roads. The chart (right) identifies the names of these toll roads, the locations of the toll plazas, points between which the toll roads stretch, and grid references for locating these roads on the maps in this book.

Toll Roads

ROUTE	PROVINCE	NAME	TOLL PLAZA	LOCATION
N1	Western Cape	HUGUENOT TUNNEL	HUGUENOT	DU TOITSKLOOF
N1	Free State	KROONVAAL	VAAL	UNCLE CHARLIES-KROONSTAD
N1	Gauteng		GRASMERE	JOHANNESBURG-VANDERBIJLPARK
N1	Limpopo	KRANSKOP	KRANSKOP	BELA-BELA-MIDDELFONTEIN
N2	Western Cape	TSITSIKAMMA	TSITSIKAMMA	THE CRAGS AND STORMS RIVER
N2	KwaZulu-Natal	SOUTH COAST	ORIBI	SOUTHBROOM-MARBURG
N2	KwaZulu-Natal		IZOTSHA	SOUTHBROOM-MARBURG
N2	KwaZulu-Natal	NORTH COAST	TONGAAT	UMDLOTI-BALLITO
N2	KwaZulu-Natal		UMVOTI	SHAKASKRAAL/KWADUKUZA
N2	KwaZulu-Natal		MTUNZINI	MTUNZINI/FELIXTON
N3	Free State	HIGHVELD	WILGE	VILLIERS-WARDEN
N3	KwaZulu-Natal	MIDLANDS	TUGELA	KEEVERSFONTEIN-FRERE
N3	KwaZulu-Natal		MOOI RIVER	FRERE-CEDARA
N3	KwaZulu-Natal	MARIANNHILL	MARIANNHILL	ASSAGAY-PINETOWN
N4	Gauteng	MAGALIES	QUAGGA	PRETORIA-ATTERIDGEVILLE
N4	Gauteng		PELINDABA	ATTERIDGEVILLE-PELINDABA
N17	Gauteng	WITWATERSRAND	DALPARK	SPRINGS-DALPARK
N17	Gauteng		DENNE ROAD	SPRINGS-DALPARK
N17	Gauteng		GOSFORTH	DALPARK-RAND AIRPORT

Climate Chart

Climate Charts

These occur throughout the atlas, and give the average temperatures and rainfall for the relevant region or city.

JOHANNESBURG	J	F	M	A	M	J	J	A	S	O	N	D
AV. TEMP. °C	20	20	18	16	13	10	10	13	16	18	18	19
AV. TEMP. °F	68	68	64	61	55	50	50	55	61	64	64	66
DAILY SUN hrs	8	8	8	8	9	9	9	10	9	9	8	8
RAINFALL mm	131	95	81	55	19	7	6	6	26	72	114	106
RAINFALL in	5.5	4	3.5	2.5	0.7	0.3	0.2	0.2	1	3	4.5	4.5

PRETORIA	J	F	M	A	M	J	J	A	S	O	N	D
AV. TEMP. °C	23	22	21	18	15	11	12	14	18	20	21	22
AV. TEMP. °F	73	72	70	64	59	52	54	57	64	68	70	73
DAILY SUN hrs	9	8	8	8	9	9	9	10	10	9	9	9
RAINFALL mm	152	76	80	57	14	3	3	6	21	67	101	105
RAINFALL in	6	3	3.5	2.5	0.6	0.1	0.1	0.2	0.8	3	4	4.5

BLOEMFONTEIN	J	F	M	A	M	J	J	A	S	O	N	D
AV. TEMP. °C	23	21	19	15	11	7	7	10	14	17	19	22
AV. TEMP. °F	73	70	66	59	52	45	45	50	57	63	66	72
DAILY SUN hrs	10	9	9	9	9	9	9	9	10	10	10	10
RAINFALL mm	91	99	74	58	21	12	9	14	19	42	59	62
RAINFALL in	4	4	3	2.5	0.8	0.5	0.3	0.6	0.7	2	2.5	2.5

DURBAN	J	F	M	A	M	J	J	A	S	O	N	D
AV. TEMP. °C	24	25	24	22	19	17	16	17	19	20	22	23
AV. TEMP. °F	75	77	75	72	66	63	61	63	66	68	72	73
DAILY SUN hrs	6	7	7	7	7	7	7	7	6	5	5	6
RAINFALL mm	135	114	124	87	64	26	44	58	65	89	104	108
RAINFALL in	5.5	4.5	5	3.5	3	1	2	2.5	3	4	4.5	4.5
SEA TEMP. °C	24	25	24	23	21	20	19	19	20	21	22	23
SEA TEMP. °F	75	77	75	73	70	68	66	66	68	70	72	73

EAST LONDON	J	F	M	A	M	J	J	A	S	O	N	D
AV. TEMP. °C	22	22	21	19	18	16	16	16	17	18	19	21
AV. TEMP. °F	72	72	70	66	64	61	61	61	63	64	66	70
DAILY SUN hrs	7	7	7	7	7	7	8	7	7	7	7	8
RAINFALL mm	74	95	106	80	55	40	51	75	93	95	90	74
RAINFALL in	3	4	4.5	3.5	2.5	2	2.5	3	4	4	4	3.5
SEA TEMP. °C	19	19	19	18	18	17	17	17	18	18	18	18
SEA TEMP. °F	66	66	66	64	64	63	63	63	64	64	64	64

PORT ELIZABETH	J	F	M	A	M	J	J	A	S	O	N	D
AV. TEMP. °C	21	21	20	18	16	14	14	14	15	17	18	20
AV. TEMP. °F	70	70	68	64	61	57	57	57	59	63	64	68
DAILY SUN hrs	9	8	7	7	7	7	7	8	7	8	9	7
RAINFALL mm	41	39	55	57	68	61	54	75	70	59	49	34
RAINFALL in	2	2	2.5	2.5	3	2.5	2.5	3	3	2.5	2	1.5
SEA TEMP. °C	21	21	20	19	17	16	16	16	17	18	19	21
SEA TEMP. °F	70	70	68	66	63	61	61	61	63	64	66	70

MOSSEL BAY	J	F	M	A	M	J	J	A	S	O	N	D
AV. TEMP. °C	21	21	20	18	17	16	15	15	16	17	18	20
AV. TEMP. °F	70	70	68	64	63	61	59	59	61	63	64	68
DAILY SUN hrs	7	7	7	7	7	7	7	7	7	7	7	7
RAINFALL mm	28	31	36	40	37	31	32	36	39	38	34	28
RAINFALL in	1	1	1.5	2	1.5	1	1	1.5	2	1.5	1.5	1
SEA TEMP. °C	22	22	20	19	18	16	16	16	17	19	19	21
SEA TEMP. °F	72	72	68	66	64	61	61	61	61	63	66	70

CAPE TOWN	J	F	M	A	M	J	J	A	S	O	N	D
AV. TEMP. °C	21	21	20	17	15	13	12	13	14	16	18	20
AV. TEMP. °F	70	70	68	63	59	55	54	55	57	61	64	68
DAILY SUN hrs	11	10	9	7	6	6	6	7	8	9	10	11
RAINFALL mm	14	17	19	39	74	92	70	75	39	37	15	17
RAINFALL in	0.6	0.7	0.7	2	3	4	3	3	2	1.5	0.6	0.7
SEA TEMP. °C	15	14	13	13	12	12	12	13	13	14	14	14
SEA TEMP. °F	59	57	55	55	54	54	54	55	55	57	57	57

LANGEBAAN	J	F	M	A	M	J	J	A	S	O	N	D
AV. TEMP. °C	17	17	17	16	15	14	13	13	14	15	16	17
AV. TEMP. °F	63	63	63	61	59	57	55	55	57	59	61	63
DAILY SUN hrs	7	6	7	7	8	8	8	7	6	7	7	7
RAINFALL mm	3	2	6	15	20	21	22	18	11	8	4	5
RAINFALL in	0.1	0	0.2	0.6	0.8	0.8	0.9	0.7	0.4	0.3	0.1	0.2
SEA TEMP. °C	15	14	13	13	12	12	12	13	13	14	14	14
SEA TEMP. °F	59	57	55	55	54	54	54	55	55	57	57	57

Legend

Motorway / Autobahn / Autoroute

National road / Nationalstrasse / Route nationale

Principal road / Regionalstrasse / Route départementale

Main road / Hauptstrasse / Route principale — Tarred   Untarrred

Minor road / Nebenstrasse / Route secondaire — Tarred   Untarrred

Route number / Routennummer / Numéro de route — N4 R 28 R518

Distance in kilometres / Entfernung in Kilometern / Distance en kilomètres — 19 15

Railway and station / Eisenbahn und Bahnhof / Chemin de fer et gare

International boundary / Internationale Grenze / Frontière internationale

Provincial boundary / Provinzgrenze / Frontière provinciale

Province name / Provinzname / Nom de la province — *KwaZulu-Natal*

Scenic route / Panoramastrasse / Route touristique

Mountain pass / Gebirgspass / Col — *Du Toitskloof*

Motorway & interchange / Autobahn und -kreuz / Autoroute avec échangeur

National reserves and parks / Nationalreservat und Park / Réserve naturelle et parc — *Mountain Zebra NP*

Airport / Flughafen / Aéroport — INT. / Other

Golf course / Golfplatz / Terrain de golf

Major petrol stop / Grosse Tankstelle / Station-service

Place of interest / Sehenswürdigkeit / Endroit à visiter — ★ *Historic Houses*

Peak in metres / Höhe in Metern / Altitude (en mètres) — Table Mtn ▲ 1140 m

Mountain range / Gebirgskette / Chaîne de montagnes

Water / Gewässer / Eau — *River, Waterfall, Swamp, Dam*

Toll road / Gebührenpflichtige Strasse / Route à péage — T

City / Grossstadt / Grande ville — ■

Major town / Kreisstadt / Ville importante — ◉

Small town / Kleinstadt / Petite ville — ○

Large village / Grössere Ortschaft / Grand village — ◎

Village / Dorf / Village — ○

Lighthouse / Leuchtturm / Phare

Border post / Grenzübergang / Frontière — Lebombo

Cave/Ruin / Höhle/Ruine / Grotte/Ruines

Hotel (selected) / Hotel (Auswahl) / Hôtel (sélectionné) — H ALBANY

Picnic site / Picknickplatz / Pique-nique

Safe bathing beach / Badestrand / Baignade autorisée

Viewpoint / Aussichtspunkt / Point de vue

Camp / Camp / Camp

Battle site / Hist. Schlachtfeld / Lieu de bataille historique — ✕ *uLundi*

Caravan park / Wohnwagenpark / Camping pour caravanes

Motorway and slip road / Autobahn mit Zufahrtsstrasse / Autoroute et bretelle d'accès

Main road and mall / Haupt- und Einkaufsstrasse / Grand rue et rue piétonnière — MALL

Road / Strasse / Route

Built-up area / Wohngebiet / Agglomération

Building of Interest / Interessantes Bauwerk / Edifice intéressant — Kruger House

Museum / Museum / Musée — Agricultural Museum

College/University / Hochschule/Universität / Collège/Université

School / Schule / École — Bergvlam High School

Church/Mosque / Kirche/Moschee / Église/Mosquée — △△

Shopping centre / Einkaufszentrum / Centre commercial — S *The Workshop*

Information Centre / Auskunftsbüro / Centre d'information — i

Parking area / Parkplatz / Parking — P

Library / Bibliothek / Bibliothèque

One-way street / Einbahnstrasse / Rue à sens-unique — →

Restaurant / Restaurant / Restaurant — R

Post office / Postamt / Bureau de poste — ✉

Bus terminus / Busbahnhof / Terminus d'autobus

Police station / Polizeirevier / Poste de police — ●

Hospital / Krankenhaus / Hôpital — ✚

Gauteng

*J*ohannesburg, bustling financial capital of Gauteng and South Africa's largest metropolis, and stately Pretoria, the country's administrative capital, are located 56km (35 miles) apart on the Highveld, the highest part of the great interior plateau. Southwest of central Johannesburg sprawls the urban conglomerate of Soweto, largest of the country's former 'African townships'; farther south is a concentration of industrial centres that includes Vereeniging and Vanderbijlpark, while to the north lie Johannesburg's affluent garden suburbs. All these form what is known as Gauteng — South Africa's pulsating economic heartland.

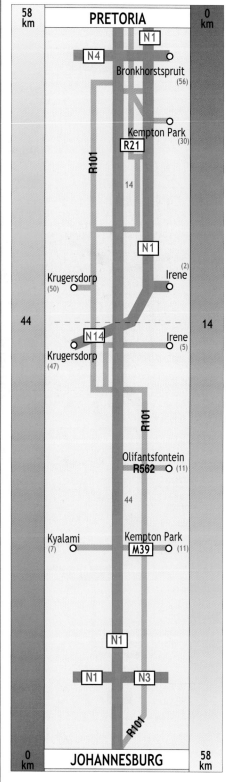

MAIN ATTRACTIONS

Johannesburg: South Africa's commercial and financial capital, a modern city dominated by concrete-and-glass giants (*see page 12*).
Pretoria: the lovely 'Jacaranda City' with a wealth of historic buildings; in October its avenues are strewn with lilac blossoms (*see page 16*).
Sterkfontein Caves: source of artefacts from the dawn of humankind, now a World Heritage Site.

Hartbeespoort Dam: picturesquely situated at the foothills of the Magaliesberg mountain range; popular with many anglers, campers and water-sports enthusiasts.
Casino Entertainment complexes: glittering venues, with much to offer besides gambling, include Sun City Resort and Casino Complex, Carnival City, Emperor's Palace, Montecasino, Gold Reef City and the Carousel.

USEFUL CONTACTS

Police, tel: 10111 (national number).
Ambulance, tel: 10177 (national number).
Charlotte Maxeke Johannesburg Hospital, tel: 011 488 4911, fax: 643 1210.
Gauteng Tourism Authority,
Airport: tel: 011 390 3602/14;
Newtown: tel: 011 639 1600.
Rosebank: tel: 011 327 2000.
Computicket, tel: 083 915 8000.
First National Bank, tel: 0860 112 244.
AA of South Africa, tel: 083 843 22.
South African Tourism, tel: 011 895 3000.
Johannesburg Tourism, tel: 011 214 0700.

TRAVEL TIPS

A network of well-signposted roads and highways links the centres in this region. Speed limits apply to usual urban zones like schools and hospitals. As in crowded city areas worldwide, crime presents a growing problem. Common sense, however, goes a long way towards preventing potentially unpleasant situations. Below are some safety guidelines:
• Plan your itinerary before setting out.
• Don't leave your vehicle if it is bumped from behind, but rather proceed to a populated and well-lit area.
• Never park in poorly lit areas.
• Don't walk around alone after dusk.
• Leave your personal belongings and valuables safely stored in the hotel when you venture out.

Below: *Designed in grandiose style, the Gold Reef City casino complex in Johannesburg contains a casino, retail outlets and a four-star hotel.*

Gauteng

Scale 1: 710 000

0   20   40 km

0   10   20 miles

N

Northam

Limpopo

POLOKWANE

Settlers

R576

15

N1

Radium

Bier

Pilanesberg National Park

PILANESBERG

Borakalalo Game Reserve

Moretele

Klipvoor Dam

Carousel Entertainment World

Rust de Winter Dam

Pienaarsrivier

Mogwase

R510

Vaalkop Dam

Assen

Atlanta

19

20

Babelegi

Temba

Boekenhout

Sun City/Lost City

21

Hex

Beestekraal

Winterveld

Soutpan

Tswaing Crater and Museum

38

R565

22

Boshoek

Krokodil

R511

Rashoop

Tswaing NR

N1

Rooikoppies Dam

Morula Sun

Soshanguve

Kwamhlanga

R573

26

Phokeng

R556

Pansdrif

Mabopane

R80

Seringkop

Royal Bafokeng Stadium

Sterkstroom

Ga-Rankuwa

Akasia

Bon Accord

N1

R101

Roodeplaat Dam NR

Roodeplaat Dam

Premier Diamond Mine

Paul Kruger's Cottage

Syringa Tree Stump

Brits

Vredesboom

R566

De Wildt

Rosslyn

Onderstepoort

R513

Bynespoort

ZEERUST

N4

Bospoort Dam

ROUTE TO SUN CITY

Sonop

R511

R513 De Wildt Cheetah Centre

R514

PRETORIA

Mamelodi

Cullinan

Rustenburg

R24

Marikana

15

2

Hartbeespoort

WATERBERGE

National Zoo

MBOMBELA NELSPRUIT

Rustenburg Nature Reserve

45

Snake Park

N4

Voortrekker Monument

Bronkhorstspruit

R52

R24

Rex

Buffelspoort Dam

Mooinooi

Hartbeespoort Dam

23

Atteridgeville

R21

Centurion

BRON MTNS

N4

MAGALIESBERG

R560

Lesedi Cultural Village

16

8

R55

Rietvlei Dam

Heldina

WITWATERSRAND

Crocodile River Ramble

Diepsloot NR

N14

R50

Rietvlei NR

Welbekend

R30

Magaliesburg Nature Area

John Nash NR

LANSERIA

N1

R21

R509

R24

Crocodile

R114

SA Lippizaner Centre

R562

Clayville

Bapsfontein

Derby

R24

Cradle of Humankind (World Heritage Site)

Kyalami Race Course

R562

Tembisa

R25

R563

Sterkfontein Caves

Lion Park

Montecasino

R564

Halfway House

R51

Magaliesburg

Oaktree

N14

R512

Muldersdrift

M71

R101

Kempton Park

R50

Walter Sisulu National Botanical Gardens

R28

Randburg

Sandton

20

N1

21

M57

OR TAMBO INTERNATIONAL

Benoni

Krugersdorp

M1

N3

R25

Emperor's Palace

N12

Krugersdorp Game Reserve

N1

JOHANNESBURG

Edenvale

R24

Boksburg

Randfontein

R24

N12

Germiston

R554

Springs

Roodepoort

R358

R33

M2

RAND

Carnival City

R29

North West

Mohlakeng

National Exhibition Centre

Gold Reef City

Alberton

R554

R21

R23

R28

Soweto

R559

N12

R554

R556

R103

Nigel

N14

R500

R41

Bekkersdal

Lenasia

R554

Katlehong

R550

R51

Westonaria

R501

R28

R558

R553

N1

R59

R550

Carletonville

Ennerdale

R558

Platberg 1841m

R3

Gauteng

R501

R28

R82

Henley-on-Klip

Perdekop 1903 m

Heidelberg

Danie Theron Monument

Fochville

R500

Evaton

R551

Meyerton

Suikerbosrand Nature Reserve

Transport Museum

R42

Sebokeng

R551

Midvaal Motor Race Track

R557

Rietpan

N12

R54

R553

R28

R54

Vereeniging

R549

Suikerbosrant

R23

N3

Potchefstroom (Tlokwe)

N1

Sharpeville

Vaal

DURBAN

KLERKSDORP

Vanderbijlpark

KROONSTAD

VRYBURG

Mooi

Greater Johannesburg

The huge yellow mine dumps and rusting headgear of the abandoned gold mines to the south of modern Johannesburg are evocative reminders of the days when the city was essentially a diggers' camp — a visit to Gold Reef City lets you relive the exciting gold-rush past. To the north, wealthy garden suburbs like Sandton and Randburg offer up-market shopping centres, fashionable boutiques, souvenir shops, an impressive range of cosmopolitan and ethnic restaurants, and numerous entertainment venues. Informal art and craft markets are regularly held in the many parks. For the golfer, there are a dozen challenging courses.

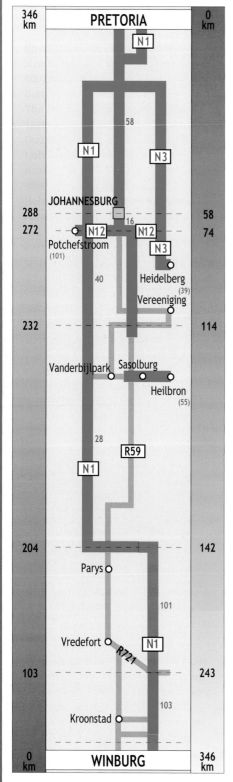

MAIN ATTRACTIONS

Gold Reef City: experience Johannesburg during the gold-rush days. Descend deep into a mine, visit the museums and the fairground, tel: 011 248 6800.
Brightwater Commons: attractive complex with live entertainment, restaurants, shops and pubs.
Market Theatre complex: theatre and jazz venue in the city centre, and the location of Newtown Art Gallery, tel: 011 832 1641.
Museum Africa: displays and artefacts illustrate South Africa's turbulent history from prehistory to the present, tel: 011 833 5624.
Flea markets: the Johannesburg (at the Market Theatre every Saturday 09:00-16:00) and Bruma Lake (daily 10:00-18:00) flea markets offer almost anything. Great for people watching.
Soweto: fascinating tours in South Africa's most famous township. For information call the Gauteng Tourism Authority, *see* page 10.

EVENTS AND FESTIVALS

South African PGA Golf Tournament: International and Southern African golfing greats meet in **Jan** to fight it out for this prestigious title.
Rand Show: in **Apr** the National Exhibition Centre (southwest of Johannesburg) hosts the biggest consumer show in Africa, featuring local and international products.
Johannesburg Pops Festival: in **Apr** traditional and contemporary musicians, choirs and soloists get together for the most vibrant three-day outdoor concert in Southern Africa.
International Eisteddfod of South Africa: during **Sep/Oct** in the city of **Roodepoort** musicians and dancers from around the world compete for honours in this cultural event.
Gay and Lesbian Pride: original, largest local gay and lesbian celebration, **Sep**.
Encounters: South Africa's only film festival devoted exclusively to documentaries; **Jul-Aug**, features screenings, panel discussions and workshops.

ACCOMMODATION

Sandton Sun and Tower, Sandton City, tel: 011 780 5000, fax: 780 5002; luxurious accommodation.
The Grace, Rosebank, tel: 011 280 7200, fax: 280 7474; small five-star hotel.
Emperor's Palace, Kempton Park, tel: 011 928 1000; luxurious, up-market casino complex.
Gold Reef Protea Hotel, tel: 011 248-5700, fax: 011 248 5791; Victorian charm, located right in the theme park.
City Lodge Morningside, tel: 011 884 9500, fax:

884 9440; just 30 minutes from the airport in lovely Sandton.
Garden Court Milpark, Auckland Park, tel: 011 726 5100, fax: 726 5123; 6km (4 miles) from the city centre.
Karos Johannesburger, tel: 011 725 3753, fax: 725 6309; located in the heart of town.
Airport Formula 1, tel: 011 392 1453, fax: 974 3845; budget; close to the International Airport.
City Lodge Airport, tel: 011 392 1750, fax: 392

2644; 5 min from airport.
The Cottages, guest-house and conference centre in Observatory, tel: 011 487 2829.
Ah Ha Guesthouse, located in Bedfordview, 15 minutes for the airport, tel: 011 616 3702.
Mama Lolo's, tel: 011 985 9183, cell: 082 332 2460; award-winning establishment where Mrs Mabitsela, a retired teacher, shares her wealth of first-hand knowledge of the turbulence in Soweto in the 70s with her guests.

Scale 1: 200 000

Greater Johannesburg

Pretoria

*H*andsome Pretoria is noted for its stately, historic homes, the impressive Union Buildings (home to major departments of the national government), its parks and gardens with their splendid wealth of flora, and for its tall jacaranda trees that transform the streets into a blaze of lilac each October/November, earning Pretoria its nickname, 'Jacaranda City'. The city is the administrative capital of the country, as well as a centre of research and learning. Within its limits lie the University of Pretoria; gigantic UNISA, among the world's largest distance-learning institutions; and Onderstepoort, an internationally renowned veterinary research institute.

Above: *Summertime in Pretoria is heralded by a glory of lilac blossoms as the many jacaranda trees begin to flower, covering city streets and walks with a fragrant, pastel-coloured carpet.*

MAIN ATTRACTIONS

Union Buildings: magnificent edifice designed by Sir Herbert Baker overlooking the city from Meintjieskop. To view the lovely gardens, tel: 012 300 5200.

Church Square: historic town square framed by beautiful old buildings such as the Ou Raadsaal (parliament), Palace of Justice and SA Reserve Bank.

Voortrekker Monument: construction on Monument Hill, 6km (4 miles) from the city, commemorating the Great Trek of the 1830 pioneers.

National Zoological Gardens: Africa's largest zoological garden and houses an array of southern African and exotic animals. The zoo is open 365 days a year, tel: 012 328 3265, www.zoo.ac.za

Transvaal Museum of Natural History: extensive displays, including the impressive 'Life's Genesis' and the Austin Roberts Bird Hall, tel: 012 322 7632, fax: 322 7939.

State Theatre: on completion in 1981, this cultural complex, comprising five theatres and a public square, was the largest of its kind in the southern hemisphere, tel: 012 392 4000, fax: 322 3913.

ACCOMMODATION

Centurion Lake Hotel, 1001 Lenchen Avenue North, Centurion, tel: 012 643 3600, fax: 643 3636.
Southern Sun Pretoria, cnr Beatrix and Church streets, Arcadia, tel: 012 341 1571, fax: 440 7534; centrally located.
Arcadia Hotel, tel: 012 326 9311, fax: 326 1067; beautifully situated right at the foot of the impressive Union Buildings.

Garden Court Hatfield, tel: 012 342 1444, fax: 342 3492.
Bentley's Country Lodge, cnr Main Street and Brits Road, Akasia, tel: 012 542 1751, fax: 542 3487.
The Farm Inn, Lynnwood Road, The Willows, tel: 012 809 0266, fax: 809 0146; beautiful game farm close to the city and the Menlyn Park shopping and entertainment centre, next to Silverlakes Golf Club.

USEFUL CONTACTS

Pretoria Tourist Information Centre, Church Square, tel: 012 337 4430.
International Embassies/Consulates, all on dialling code 012:
- Australia, tel: 423 6000, fax: 342 4222
- France, tel: 425 1600, fax: 425 1609
- Germany, tel: 427 8900, fax: 343 9401
- Italy, tel: 423 0000, fax: 430 5547
- Netherlands, tel: 425 4500
- Spain, tel: 344 3875-7, fax: 343 4891
- UK, tel: 421 7500, fax: 421 7555
- USA, tel: 431 4000, fax: 342 2299.

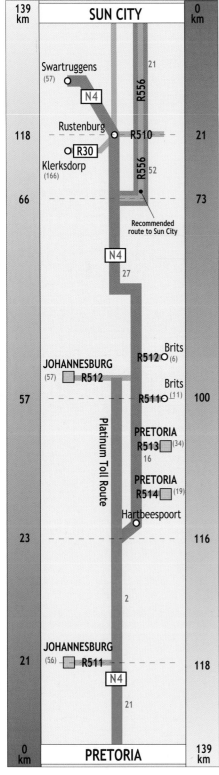

139 km	SUN CITY	0 km
	21	
Swartruggens (57)	R556	
	N4	
118	Rustenburg R510	21
	R30	
	R556 52	
Klerksdorp (166)		
66		73
	Recommended route to Sun City	
	N4	
	27	
	Brits R512 (6)	
JOHANNESBURG (57) R512		
	Brits	
57	R511 (11)	100
	PRETORIA R513 (34) 16	
Platinum Toll Route	PRETORIA R514 (19)	
	Hartbeespoort	
23		116
	2	
21	JOHANNESBURG (56) R511	118
	N4	
	21	
0 km	PRETORIA	139 km

Pilanesberg and Sun City

*T*he dramatic Lost City and Sun City leisure resort, one of South Africa's most glittering tourist venues featuring casinos, bars, restaurants, hotels, theatres, nightclubs and shops, is set among the lush vegetation of beautifully landscaped grounds, in what before was little more than desert territory. Apart from the 31,500m² (339,063ft²) Valley of the Waves, a man-made water park with soft sand beaches, waterslides, cascades and 1.8m-high (5.9ft) waves, the complex also offers an Arizona Desert-style golf course where crocodiles lie in wait at the 13th hole, and another at the Gary Player Country Club, venue of the annual Nedbank Golf Challenge. Musicians such as Queen and Elton John have also performed at the Sun City Super Bowl, a large auditorium which seats 6000. Pilanesberg National Park north of Sun City has some 10,000 head of wildlife including the Big Five — buffalo, rhino (black and white), elephant, lion and leopard — and over 300 bird species. This game-rich habitat lies within four concentric mountain rings, the relics of an ancient volcano. In the centre of the bowl is Mankwe Dam, a favourite hippo haunt. The park is traversed by a network of game-viewing roads; guided walks and drives are conducted and hot-air balloon trips can be organized. This wonderful park is the result of 'Operation Genesis', a successful game-stocking venture. A visit to the aviary at Manyane Gate should not be missed.

ACCOMMODATION

Sun City complex, tel: 014 557 1000.
The Cascades Hotel, tel: 014 557 5840.
Palace of the Lost City Hotel, tel: 014 557 4307. Luxurious extravagance.
The Cabanas Hotel, tel: 014 557 1580. Family orientated and affordable.
Sun City Hotel, tel: 014 557 5110. Five-star comfort surrounded by sub-tropical gardens.

Pilanesberg National Park, tel: 014 555 1600.
Bakubung Game Lodge, tel: 014 552 6000, fax: 552 6300; thatched rooms around a hippo pool in a private game reserve.
Kwa Maritane Lodge, tel: 014 552 5100, fax: 552 5333; luxurious accommodation in the African bush.

USEFUL CONTACTS

Pilanesberg National Park, tel: 014 555 1600; for the real bush experience.

Below: *Fabled to be the royal residence of an ancient king, the Palace of the Lost City rises dramatically out of the surrounding African bush, like the legendary temple of a mysterious civilization.*

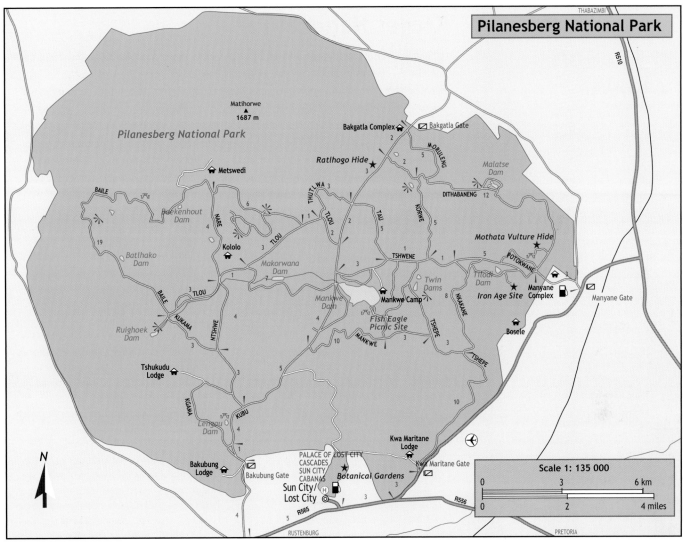

Pilanesberg National Park

Pilanesberg National Park

Matlhorwe ▲ 1687 m

Metswedi

Bakgatla Complex · Bakgatla Gate

Ratlhogo Hide ★

Boekenhout Dam

Kololo

Makorwana Dam

Mankwe Dam

Mankwe Camp

Twin Dams

Mothata Vulture Hide ★

Iron Age Site ★ · Manyane Complex · Manyane Gate

Batlhako Dam

Fish Eagle Picnic Site

Bosele

Ruighoek Dam

Tshukudu Lodge

Lengau Dam

Kwa Maritane Lodge

Kwa Maritane Gate

PALACE OF LOST CITY CASCADES SUN CITY CABANAS

Botanical Gardens

Bakubung Lodge · Bakubung Gate

Sun City/ Lost City

THABAZIMBI

R510

MORULENG

DITHABANENG · Malatse Dam

POTOKWANE

Titodi Dam

RUSTENBURG

PRETORIA

R565 · R556

Scale 1: 135 000

0 — 3 — 6 km
0 — 2 — 4 miles

N

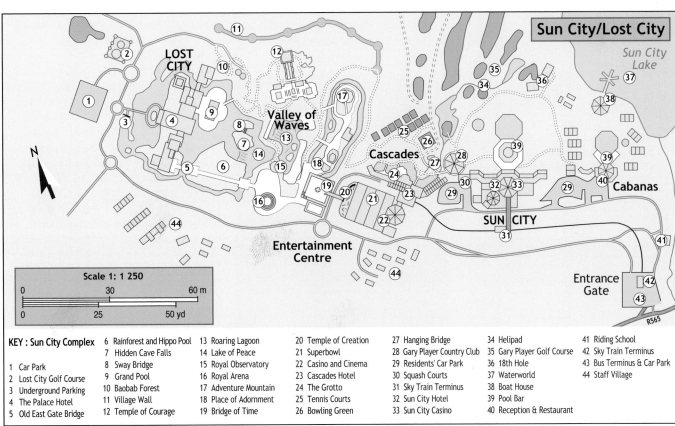

Sun City/Lost City

LOST CITY

Valley of Waves

Cascades

SUN CITY

Cabanas

Sun City Lake

Entertainment Centre

Entrance Gate

R565

Scale 1: 1 250

0 — 30 — 60 m
0 — 25 — 50 yd

N

KEY : Sun City Complex

1 Car Park	6 Rainforest and Hippo Pool	13 Roaring Lagoon
2 Lost City Golf Course	7 Hidden Cave Falls	14 Lake of Peace
3 Underground Parking	8 Sway Bridge	15 Royal Observatory
4 The Palace Hotel	9 Grand Pool	16 Royal Arena
5 Old East Gate Bridge	10 Baobab Forest	17 Adventure Mountain
	11 Village Wall	18 Place of Adornment
	12 Temple of Courage	19 Bridge of Time

20 Temple of Creation	27 Hanging Bridge	34 Helipad	41 Riding School
21 Superbowl	28 Gary Player Country Club	35 Gary Player Golf Course	42 Sky Train Terminus
22 Casino and Cinema	29 Residents' Car Park	36 18th Hole	43 Bus Terminus & Car Park
23 Cascades Hotel	30 Squash Courts	37 Waterworld	44 Staff Village
24 The Grotto	31 Sky Train Terminus	38 Boat House	
25 Tennis Courts	32 Sun City Hotel	39 Pool Bar	
26 Bowling Green	33 Sun City Casino	40 Reception & Restaurant	

Kruger National Park

*S*outh Africa's premier wildlife sanctuary covers more than 20,000 km² (7720 sq miles) — an area about the size of Wales and larger than the state of Israel. Because this vast, wild expanse encompasses many different habitats, it is a haven for more varieties of wildlife than any other conservation area in Africa. Among the estimated 140 mammal species occurring here are the Big Five: lion (approximately 1500), elephant (about 13,500), leopard (around 1000), buffalo (27,000), and rhino, both black and white. Other large wildlife populations include zebra, wildebeest, giraffe, hippo and crocodile, as well as some 500 bird species. If you are lucky, you may even spot a pack of the increasingly rare wild dogs.

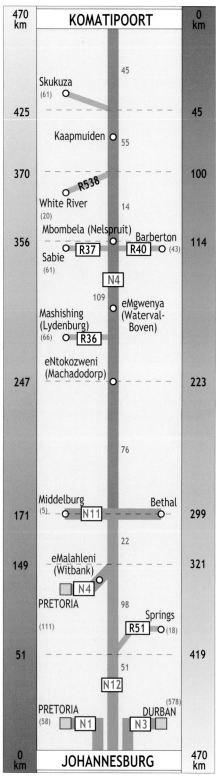

TRAVEL TIPS

An extensive network, consisting of about 880km (550 miles) of tarred surface and 1700km (1060 miles) of gravel road, traverses the park, providing effective access to all areas of the Kruger. Should you experience any car trouble, vehicle breakdown services are available at Skukuza and Letaba camps. A few general safety guidelines have to be observed by all visitors:

• Malaria treatment should be started prior to entering this area (consult your physician), and use insect repellent.
• Stay on the designated roads or tracks.
• Keep to the speed limit.
• Do not leave your vehicle.
• Don't injure, feed or disturb wildlife.
• Littering is an offence.
• Be sure to arrive at your rest camp by the stipulated time before sunset.

MAIN ATTRACTIONS

The Big Five can be viewed in their natural environment. To view, try the **Pafuri area** in the far north. **Water holes** attract a steady parade of wildlife. Overnight visitors have a choice of 20 or so comfortable, tree-shaded **rest camps,** of which **Skukuza** is the largest, boasting all the amenities of a small town. **Olifants Camp,** perched on high cliffs, offers splendid vistas. Smaller and more intimate are the **bush camps. Tshokwane** is among several attractive **picnic spots; Nwanetsi,** which overlooks the Sweni River, is an especially rewarding **look-out post.** A number of **wilderness trails** offer the ultimate bush experience. **Private game lodges** provide luxury, personal service and superb game-viewing. Popular spots include Sabi Sabi, Londolozi and Mala Mala. Check out the following website for a list of lodges in the area, www.places.co.za

Left: *Elephants should always be approached with caution. Warning signals, which include a raised trunk and flapping ears, should never be ignored. Elephants are voracious feeders which daily consume up to 272kg (600 lb) of grass, tender shoots and bark from trees. The elephant's sensitive trunk can even detect water underground. An adult elephant can drink up to 200 litres of water in a single session.*

ACCOMMODATION

Over 20 pleasant, clean and safe rest camps are located within the park. For reservations contact **South African National Parks,** tel: 012 428 9111, fax: 426 5500, website: www.sanparks.org

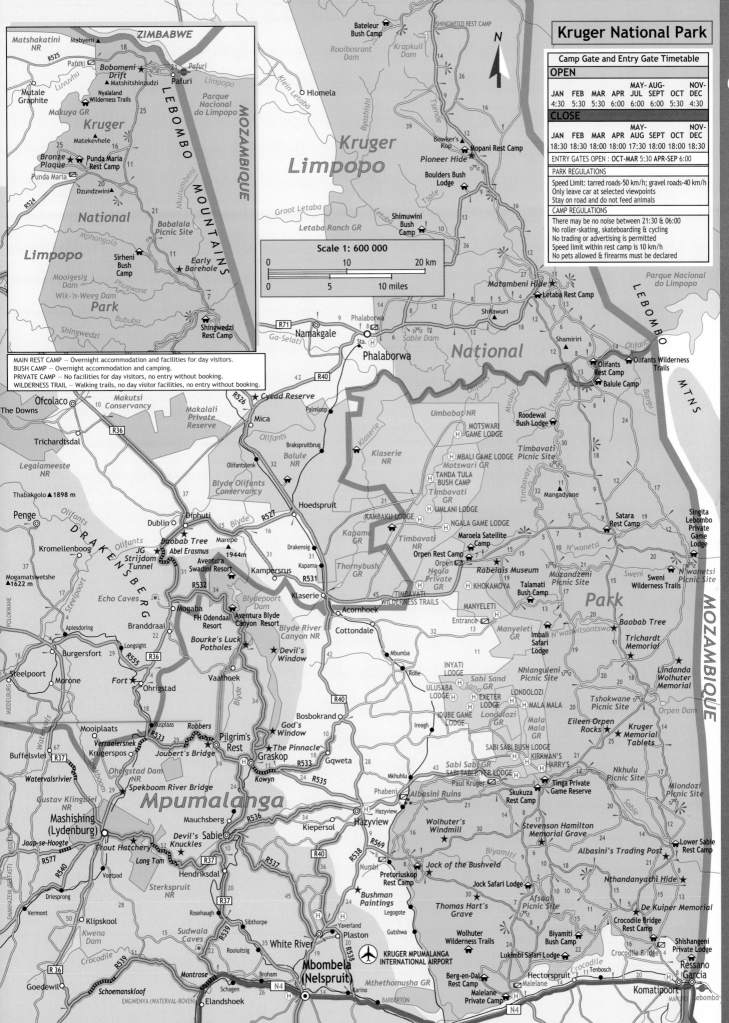

Kruger National Park

Camp Gate and Entry Gate Timetable

OPEN

	JAN	FEB	MAR	APR	MAY–JUL	AUG–SEPT	OCT	NOV–DEC
	4:30	5:30	5:30	6:00	6:00	6:00	5:30	4:30

CLOSE

	JAN	FEB	MAR	APR	MAY–AUG	SEPT	OCT	NOV–DEC
	18:30	18:30	18:00	18:00	17:30	18:00	18:00	18:30

ENTRY GATES OPEN : OCT–MAR 5:30 APR–SEP 6:00

PARK REGULATIONS
Speed Limit: tarred roads–50 km/h; gravel roads–40 km/h
Only leave car at selected viewpoints
Stay on road and do not feed animals

CAMP REGULATIONS
There may be no noise between 21:30 & 06:00
No roller-skating, skateboarding & cycling
No trading or advertising is permitted
Speed limit within rest camp is 10 km/h
No pets allowed & firearms must be declared

Scale 1 : 600 000

MAIN REST CAMP — Overnight accommodation and facilities for day visitors.
BUSH CAMP — Overnight accommodation and camping.
PRIVATE CAMP — No facilities for day visitors, no entry without booking.
WILDERNESS TRAIL — Walking trails, no day visitor facilities, no entry without booking.

Mpumalanga Drakensberg

*M*ountainous terrain, misty forests, bushveld and endless views are the compelling features of this escarpment region far to the east of Gauteng, across the great Highveld plateau. For sheer scenic beauty, few parts of the Southern African subcontinent can compare with the Great Escarpment, a spectacular wonderland of buttresses, sculpted peaks and deep ravines. The Olifants and Crocodile rivers and a score of their tributaries run through verdant valleys. One tributary, the Blyde River, over centuries carved a canyon that now ranks as one of Africa's great scenic splendours.

TRAVEL TIPS

The region has an excellent network of roads. Travelling from Johannesburg to Mbombela (Nelspruit) and the escarpment, take the R22 and then the N4 near eMalahleni (Witbank); from Pretoria take the N4 direct. The R40 leads from Mbombela (Nelspruit) north into the escarpment. Alternatively, follow the N1 national highway from Pretoria; turn right at Polokwane on the R71 for Tzaneen and the central region of the Kruger National Park (around Phalaborwa). If you're going to the far northern region of the park, take the R524 at Louis Trichardt (Makhado). Please note: this is a malaria area so ensure that the necessary precautions are taken before travelling into this area; for more information on the hazards, consult your physician.

ACCOMMODATION

Mount Sheba Hotel, west of Pilgrim's Rest, tel: 013 768 1241, fax: 768 1248; luxury hotel.
Sabi River Sun, close to Paul Kruger Gate, tel: 013 737 7311, fax: 737 7314; 18-hole golf course.
Pine Lake Lifestyle Resort, White River, tel: 013 750 0709, fax: 751 3873; on the edge of a lake; golf course.
Royal Hotel, Pilgrim's Rest, tel: 013 768 1100, fax: 768 1188; stay in a national monument.
Critchley Hackle Lodge, Dullstroom, tel: 013 254 0149, fax: 254 0262.
Malapo Country Lodge, Mashishing (Lydenburg), tel: 013 235 1056, fax: 013 235 2398; with ASTRO Boma (open-air Observatory) where African star lore comes alive.

MAIN ATTRACTIONS

Blyde River Canyon: a majestic gorge whose sheer cliff faces plunge to the water far below.
Bourke's Luck Potholes: a fantasia of hollowed-out rocks.
Pilgrim's Rest: town born out of the 1870 gold rush, now a quaint living museum.
Jock of the Bushveld: trail begins in Graskop for the heroic dog in the novel by Sir Percy FitzPatrick.
God's Window: for the most magnificent views of the area.
Mount Sheba: beautiful forest reserve high in the mountains.
Magoebaskloof: large tracts of thick indigenous forest.
Long Tom Pass: between Sabie and Mashishing (Lydenburg); spectacular.
Echo Caves: archaeological evidence of earlier inhabitants.
The Trout Triangle: area around eMgwenya (Waterval-Boven), Dullstroom and Mashishing (Lydenburg); popular with nature-lovers and the fly-fishing elite.
Khamai Reptile Park: with snakes, lizards and crocodiles. Interesting presentations and commentaries and the chance of handling a snake.

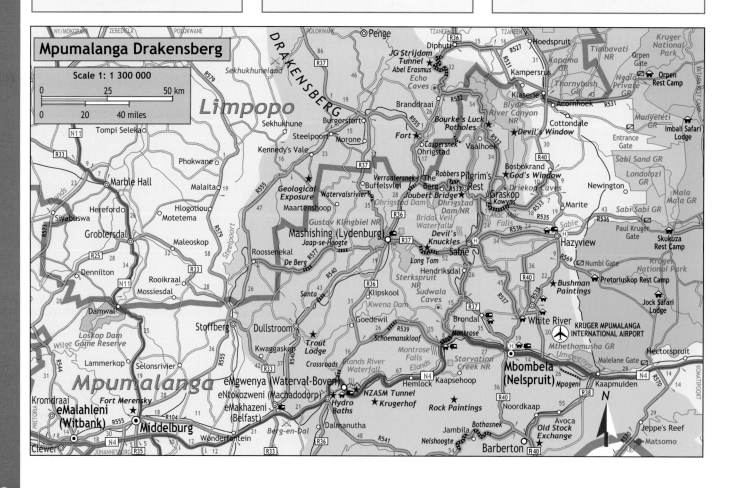

Mbombela (Nelspruit)

*L*argest town in, and capital of, Mpumalanga is Mbombela (Nelspruit), set on the Crocodile River in the warm, undulating grasslands below the escarpment and centre of a beautiful and immensely fertile area. It's an attractive little city of wide streets lined with poinciana trees that, during the summer months, are ablaze with deep red blossoms. Mbombela (Nelspruit) is the last major town on the southern route to the Kruger National Park; among its attractions are excellent hotels and restaurants, modern shopping centres and speciality outlets that cater well for the tourist.

MAIN ATTRACTIONS

Lowveld Botanical Gardens: on the Crocodile River, supporting over 600 species of indigenous flora.
Lowveld Herbarium: adjacent to the Gardens; of interest to the botanist as well as the layperson.
Sudwala Caves: dramatic cave formations and an interesting dinosaur park, about 40km (25 miles) northwest of Nelspruit.
Riverside Trail: self-guided 4km (2.5-mile) hike along the Crocodile River, with some lovely waterfalls.
Farm stalls: roadside stalls around the town sell fresh fruit and curios.
Barberton Museum Complex: opened in 1994; gives a comprehensive picture of the history, geology, archaeology and ethnology of the region.

ACCOMMODATION

Cybele Forest Lodge, R40, White River, tel: 013 764 1823, fax: 764 9510; exclusive retreat surrounded by nature.
Protea Hotel The Winkler, tel: 013 751 5068, fax: 751 5044; White River area.
Mercure Premier Lodge, Graniet Street, Mbombela (Nelspruit), tel: 013 741 4222.
The Rest Country Lodge, tel: 013 744 9991, fax: 744 9472; luxury suites near Mbombela (Nelspruit).
Lowveld Lodge, Tom Lawrence Street, White River, tel: 013 750 0206.

USEFUL CONTACTS

Mpumalanga Tourism and Parks Agency, tel: 013 752 7001.

WATERFALL ROUTE

There are some beautiful waterfalls in the Sabie-Graskop area about 50km (31 miles) north of Mbombela (Nelspruit). The falls are worth a visit and are easily accessible on a good road network. Among the best falls to view are:
Bridal Veil: a delicate spray of water surrounded by a forest echoing with the calls of many birds; 7km (4.2 miles) north of Sabie.
Mac Mac: twin cascades plunge 56m (185ft) into a deep, green ravine.
Lone Creek: hidden some 68m (222ft) in a beautiful, misty forest.
Horseshoe: a national monument.
Berlin: plunges about 48m (158ft) into a deep pool.
Lisbon: picturesque double waterfall in a setting of special beauty.

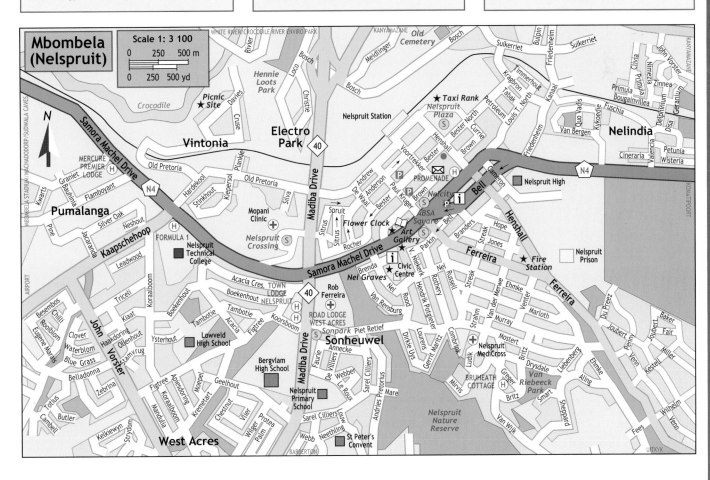

KwaZulu-Natal North Coast

*R*emarkable for its rich fauna and flora, northern KwaZulu-Natal boasts some of South Africa's finest game reserves (among them the Hluhluwe and iMfolozi Game Reserves, oldest of South Africa's many wildlife sanctuaries) and one of the world's great wetland and marine conservation areas, now a World Heritage Site, the iSimangaliso Wetland Park (St Lucia). Just north of Durban, along the Dolphin Coast that stretches for 90km (55 miles) up to the uThukela River mouth, lies the up-market resort town of uMhlanga Rocks. Beyond lies the area historically known as Zululand, whose largest centre and industrial hub is Richards Bay, notable for its busy deep-water harbour. The beaches, fringed by tropical vegetation, attract sun-bathers, anglers, divers and boating enthusiasts.

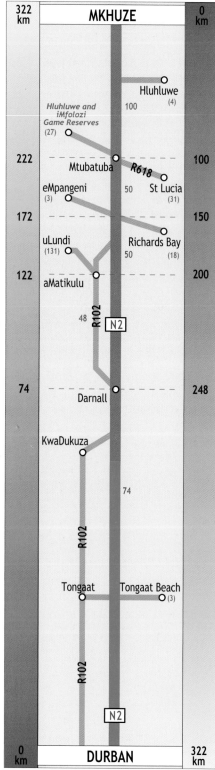

MAIN ATTRACTIONS

Beaches: some excellent beaches north and south of Durban include uMhlanga Rocks, Tongaat, Ballito, Shaka's Rock, Salt Rock, Shelly Beach, North Beach (Margate) and uVongo.

Natal Sharks Board: in uMhlanga; enjoy an informative audiovisual presentation. Book in advance.

Lake Sibaya: South Africa's largest natural freshwater lake.

The Elephant Coast: declared a World Heritage Site and among the world's most ecologically diverse sanctuaries. Contact St Lucia Tourism Association, tel: 035 590 1247.

Maputaland Reserves: host some of the greatest concentrations of wildlife in South Africa.

The **Hluhluwe and iMfolozi Game Reserves:** famed for their rhino conservation programme and offering a haven for the Big Five, tel: 035 562 0848 (Hilltop Camp), tel: 035 550 8476 (Mpila Camp).

Phinda Resource Reserve: one of the best ecotourism destinations in South Africa, tel: 035 562 0271, fax: 562 0399.

Sodwana Bay: marine wonderland, the best diving venue in South Africa, tel: 035 571 0051/2/3.

Shakaland: model of a traditional Zulu village in the Nkwaleni Valley; includes culinary specialities, tribal dancing and traditional healers. Protea Hotel Shakaland: tel: 035 460 0912.

TRAVEL TIPS

The N2 runs parallel to, but mostly out of sight of, the coast to the eMpangeni-Richards Bay area (north of Durban), and then sweeps inland to the Swaziland border. Major roads in Zululand are tarred; most of the minor ones (including those in the game reserves) are gravel and generally in a satisfactory condition.

USEFUL CONTACTS

Dolphin Coast Publicity Association, tel: 032 946 1997.

Isle of Capri Cruises, tel: 031 337 7751, fax: 031 305 3099; deep-sea cruises and fishing trips.

Natal Sharks Board, tel: 031 566 0400, fax: 031 566 0499.

Below: *The golden sands of St Lucia.*

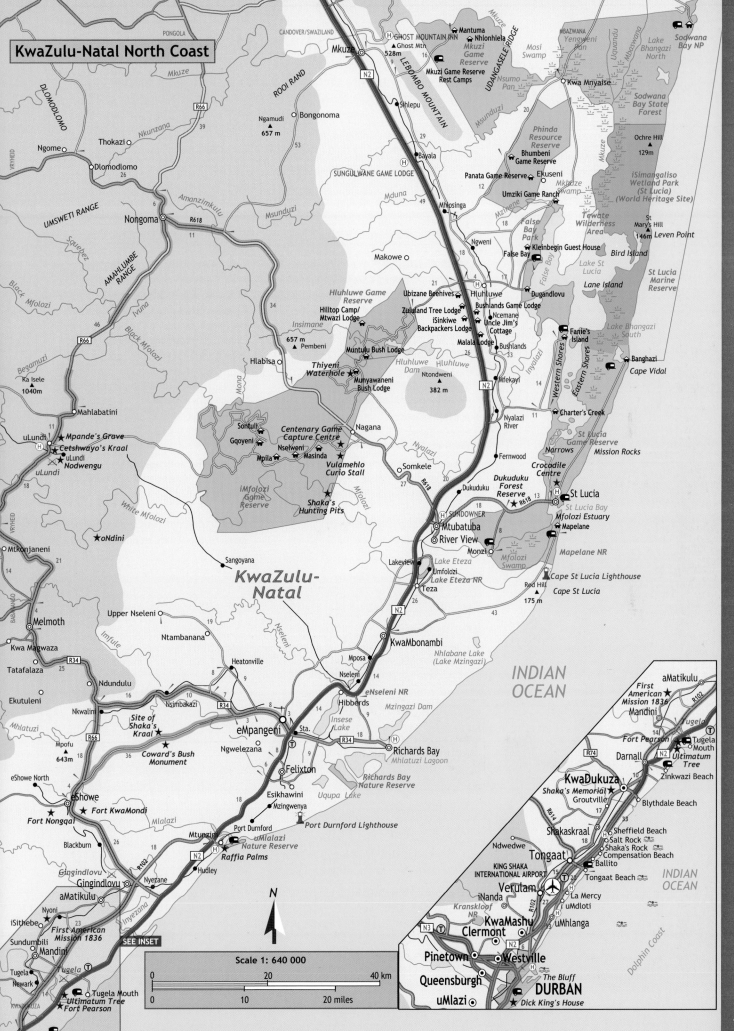

KwaZulu-Natal North Coast

PONGOLA
CANDOVER/SWAZILAND
DLOMODLOMO
Ngome
Thokazi
Dlomodlomo
UMSWETI RANGE
AMAHLUMBE RANGE
Nongoma
Mahlabatini
Ka Isele 1040 m
uLundi
Mpande's Grave
Cetshwayo's Kraal
uLundi Nodwengu
uLundi
oNdini
Mtkonjaneni
Melmoth
Kwa Magwaza
Tatafalaza
Ndundulu
Ekutuleni
Nkwalini
Mpofu 643 m
Site of Shaka's Kraal
Coward's Bush Monument
eShowe North
eShowe
Fort KwaMondi
Fort Nongqai
Blackburn
Gingindlovu
aMatikulu
Nyoni
iSithebe
First American Mission 1836
Sundumbili
Mandini
Tugela
Newark
Tugela Mouth
Ultimatum Tree
Fort Pearson
KWADUKUZA

Mkuze
Ngamudi 657 m
Bongonoma
Bayala
SUNGULWANE GAME LODGE
Makowe
Hluhluwe Game Reserve
Hilltop Camp/ Mtwazi Lodge
Insimane
657 m Pembeni
Hlabisa
Thiyeni Waterhole
Munyawaneni Bush Lodge
Sontuli
Gqoyeni
Centenary Game Capture Centre
Nselweni
Mpila Masinda
Vulamehlo Curio Stall
iMfolozi Game Reserve
Shaka's Hunting Pits
Muntulu Bush Lodge
Nagana
Somkele
Sangoyana
KwaZulu-Natal
Upper Nseleni
Ntambanana
Heatonville
Nseleni
eNseleni NR
Hibberds
Insese Lake
Mposa
eMpangeni
Ngwelezana
Felixton
Esikhawini
Mzingwenya
Port Durnford
Mtunzini
uMlalazi Nature Reserve
Raffia Palms
Hudley
Nyezane

GHOST MOUNTAIN INN
Ghost Mtn 528 m
Mantuma
Nhlonhlela
Mkuzi Game Reserve
Mkuzi Game Reserve Rest Camps
Sihlepu
LEBOMBO MOUNTAIN
UDANGASELE RIDGE
MBAZWANA
Yengweni Pan
Mosi Swamp
Kwa Mnyaise
Sodwana Bay NP
Sodwana Bay State Forest
Mduna
Bhumbeni Game Reserve
Ekuseni
Panata Game Reserve
Umziki Game Ranch
Mhlosinga
Phinda Resource Reserve
Mkhuze Swamp
iSimangaliso Wetland Park (St Lucia) (World Heritage Site)
Ochre Hill 129 m
Ngweni
Mzinene
False Bay Park
Tewate Wilderness Area
St Mary's Hill 146 m
Leven Point
Ubizane Beehives
Hluhluwe
Kleinbegin Guest House
Bird Island
Zululand Tree Lodge
Bushlands Game Lodge
Dugandlovu
False Bay
Lake St Lucia
St Lucia Marine Reserve
iSinkiwe Backpackers Lodge
Ncemane
Uncle Jim's Cottage
Lane Island
Malala Lodge
Bushlands
Ntondweni
Hluhluwe Dam
Hluhluwe
382 m
Mfekayi
Fanie's Island
Lake Bhangazi South
Banghazi
Cape Vidal
Western Shores
Eastern Shores
Charter's Creek
Nyalazi River
St Lucia Game Reserve
Mission Rocks
Narrows
Fernwood
Crocodile Centre
St Lucia
St Lucia Bay
Dukuduku
Dukuduku Forest Reserve
SUNDOWNER
Mtubatuba
River View
Monzi
Mfolozi Estuary
Mapelane
Lakeview
Lake Eteza
Umfolozi
Lake Eteza NR
Teza
Mfolozi Swamp
Cape St Lucia Lighthouse
Cape St Lucia
Red Hill 175 m
KwaMbonambi
Nhlabane Lake (Lake Mzingazi)
INDIAN OCEAN
Mzingazi Dam
Richards Bay
Mhlatuzi Lagoon
Richards Bay Nature Reserve
Uqupa Lake
Port Durnford Lighthouse

SEE INSET

N

Scale 1: 640 000
0   20   40 km
0   10   20 miles

Inset

aMatikulu
First American Mission 1836
Mandini
Fort Pearson
Tugela Mouth
Ultimatum Tree
Darnall
Zinkwazi Beach
KwaDukuza
Shaka's Memorial
Groutville
Blythdale Beach
Shakaskraal
Sheffield Beach
Salt Rock
Shaka's Rock
Compensation Beach
Ndwedwe
Ballito
Tongaat
Tongaat Beach
KING SHAKA INTERNATIONAL AIRPORT
Verulam
iNanda
La Mercy
uMdloti
Kranskloof NR
uMhlanga
KwaMashu
Clermont
Dolphin Coast
INDIAN OCEAN
N3
Pinetown
Westville
Queensburgh
uMlazi
The Bluff
DURBAN
Dick King's House

KwaZulu-Natal South Coast

*T*he seaboard running south from Durban to the Eastern Cape border, or Mtamvuna River, is known as the South Coast. It is one of the southern hemisphere's most entrancing holiday regions, a subtropical wonderland of wide, unspoilt beaches lapped by the warm blue waters of the Indian Ocean, of a lushly green hinterland, and of a score and more sunlit towns, villages and hamlets, each with its special personality and attractions. Part of the long shoreline, which runs from Hibberdene to Port Edward, is also referred to as the Hibiscus Coast.

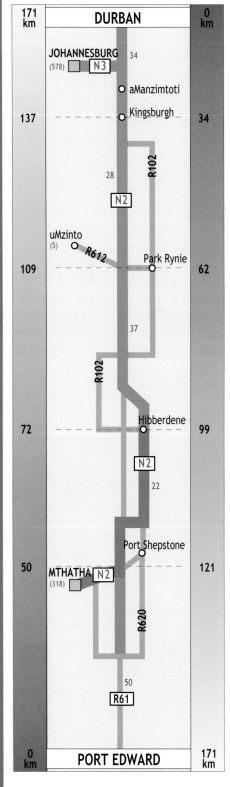

MAIN ATTRACTIONS

South Coast
Kingsburgh: five seaside resorts popular for their white sands and shark-protected bathing.
uMkomaas: a championship golf course and floodlit tidal pool.
Scottburgh: a charming beach, and fascinating Crocworld nearby.
Vernon Crookes Nature Reserve: lush sanctuary for various antelope.
Hibiscus Coast
Hibberdene: lagoon, woodland-fringed beaches, amusement park.
uMzumbe: excellent family hotel; rock and surf angling.
Banana Beach: safe bathing and very good surfing.
Bendigo: four seaside resorts geared towards holiday-makers.

uMtentweni: for a quiet getaway.
Port Shepstone: at the mouth of the Mzimkulu River; offers excellent bowling greens and one of South Africa's best golf courses.
Oribi Gorge Nature Reserve: some 20km (14 miles) inland from Port Shepstone — a striking canyon carved through layers of sandstone by the Mzimkulwana River.
uVongo: lively little resort in an idyllic tropical setting.
Margate: very popular seaside town, but it can get crowded.
Ramsgate: magnificent lagoon and a long beach.
Port Edward: charming town in the former Transkei, with a pleasant beach; close to the Wild Coast Sun.

Above: *Scottburgh is a popular holiday resort on the South Coast. The lovely beach offers safe bathing, as well as some fine angling spots.*

USEFUL CONTACTS

GJ Crookes Hospital, Scottburgh, tel: 039 976 1300.
Hibiscus Coast Tourism, Margate, tel: 039 312 2322, fax: 312 1886.
Scottburgh Tourism, tel: 039 976 1364, fax: 978 3114.

TRAVEL TIPS

Towns and resorts are linked to Durban by the N2 as far as Port Shepstone, while the R61 leads to Port Edward. Both roads are in good condition, though inland roads can be a little rough and caution is advised.

KwaZulu-Natal South Coast

Scale 1 : 640 000

Durban and Pietermaritzburg

*T*he city of Durban is South Africa's third largest metropolis, foremost seaport (the harbour is ranked ninth in the world in terms of size and traffic) and among the country's most popular holiday destinations. Durban and its subtropical surrounds offer many varied attractions: the beachfront, known as the Golden Mile, with its superb beaches (protected by anti-shark nets) for sunbathing, swimming and surfing; hotels, nightspots, restaurants, glittering shopping malls, pleasant parks and, in parts, an appealingly exotic atmosphere conferred by the city's large Indian community.

ACCOMMODATION

Royal Hotel, 267 Anton Lembede Street, tel: 031 333 6000, fax: 333 6002; one of the best hotels in Durban; very luxurious.
The Durban Hilton International, 12-14 Walnut Road, tel: 031 336 8100. One of Durban's most luxurious hotels.
Holiday Inn Garden Court South Beach, tel: 031 337 2231, fax: 337 4640; stylish and comfortable.
Holiday Inn Garden Court Marine Parade, tel: 031 337 3341, fax: 332 9885.
Balmoral Hotel, Durban Beachfront, tel: 031 368 5940, fax: 368 5955; right across the road from the beach.
Protea Hotel Imperial, 224 Jabu Ndlovu Street, Pietermaritzburg, tel: 033 342 6551, fax: 342 9796; central; colonial atmosphere.
Crossways Country Inn, Old Howick Road, just north of Pietermaritzburg, tel: 033 343 3267, fax: 343 3273; English pub atmosphere.
Rawdon's, Old Main Road, Nottingham Road, tel: 033 266 6044, fax: 266 6048; exquisite English country-style homestead.

MAIN ATTRACTIONS

Golden Mile: fabulous holiday playground stretching along the sandy Indian Ocean shoreline.
uShaka Marine World: on the Golden Mile, popular aquarium-dolphinarium, tel: 031 328 8000.
Victoria Street Indian Market: colourful and exotic place of bargain and barter.
uMgeni River Bird Park: rated third best of the world's bird parks, tel: 031 579 4600.
Gandhi Settlement: visit the renovated farm where Gandhi once resided; situated in iNanda.

Gateway shopping centre: located 10 minutes north of Durban. Here you can surf, rockclimb, enjoy a meal and, of course, shop.
Port Natal Maritime Museum: on the Victoria Embankment; interesting exhibits dealing with the city's seafaring tradition, tel: 031 311 2231, fax 311 2230.
Pietermaritzburg: this quaint colonial-style town has some fine architecture as well as interesting museums. It is home to two internationally renowned sports events, the Dusi Canoe Marathon and the Comrades Marathon.

EVENTS AND FESTIVALS

Howick: Midmar Mile swim marathon, held in **January**, sometimes **February**.
Comrades Marathon: famous marathon in **June** (Durban to Pietermaritzburg the one year, vice versa the following one).
Durban July Handicap: prestigious horse-racing event in **July**.
Mr Price Pro: world-renowned annual surfing contest held at New Pier in **June/July**.

USEFUL CONTACTS

Addington Hospital, tel: 031 327 2000, fax: 368 3300.
Durban Tourism, Tourist Junction, 160 Monty Naicker Road, Durban, tel: 031 366 7500.
uShaka Marine World, the Point, Durban, tel: 031 328 8000, www.ushakamarineworld.co.za
Pietermaritzburg Tourism, tel: 033 345 1348, fax: 394 3535.

Right: *The Paddling Pools form part of Durban's sparkling Golden Mile. Other attractions on offer here include colourful markets, numerous restaurants, scenic walkways and fountains.*

TRAVEL TIPS

Durban's international airport is 15 minutes from the city centre. It is linked to all other major South African centres by a network of national roads. The N2 leads south and then west along the coast, through Port Elizabeth to Cape Town. The N3 takes the traveller northwest through Pietermaritzburg and Harrismith to Johannesburg.

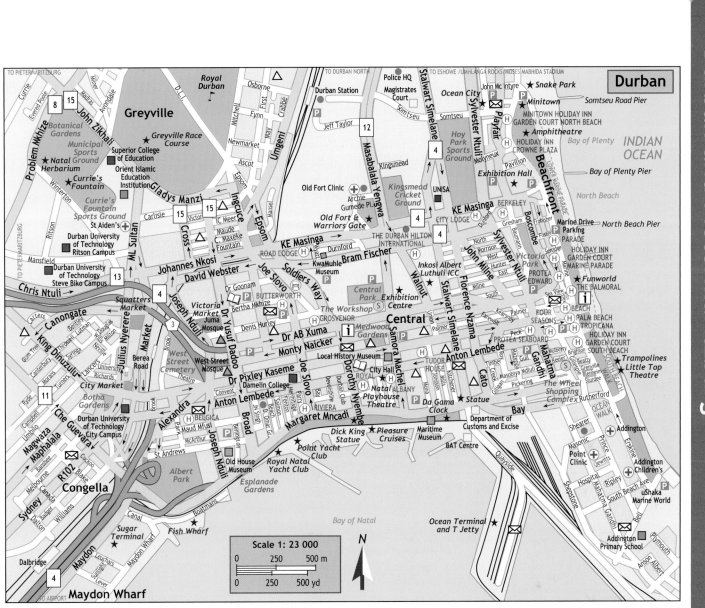

Durban

TO PIETERMARITZBURG · Royal Durban · TO DURBAN NORTH · TO ESHOWE/UMHLANGA ROCKS/MOSES MABHIDA STADIUM

Greyville · Botanical Gardens · Municipal Sports Ground · ★ Natal Herbarium · Currie's Fountain · Currie's Fountain Sports Ground · St Aiden's · Durban University of Technology Ritson Campus · Durban University of Technology Steve Biko Campus · Chris Ntuli

Greyville Race Course · Superior College of Education · Orient Islamic Education Institution · Squatters' Market · Victoria Market · Juma Mosque · West Street Cemetery · Berea Road · Botha Gardens · City Market · Durban University of Technology City Campus · Congella

Canongate · King Dinuzulu · Magwaza Maphalala · Che Guevara · R102 · Alexandra · Albert Park · Congella · Sugar Terminal · Fish Wharf · Dalbridge · Maydon · TO AIRPORT · Maydon Wharf

Royal Durban · Durban Station · Jeff Taylor · Old Fort Clinic · Archie Gumede Pl. · Old Fort & Warriors Gate · THE DURBAN HILTON INTERNATIONAL · ROAD LODGE · KwaMuhle Museum · BUTTERWORTH · Bertha Mkhize · Dr Goonam · Dr Yusuf Dadoo · Denis Hurley · Dr AB Xuma · Monty Naicker · West Street Mosque · Dr Pixley Kaseme · Damelin College · Anton Lembede · Margaret Mncadi

Police HQ · Magistrates Court · Ocean City · Hoy Park Sports Ground · UNISA · Kingsmead Cricket Ground · KE Masinga · CITY LODGE · Inkosi Albert Luthuli ICC · Central Park · Exhibition Centre · GROSVENOR · The Workshop · Medwood Gardens · Local History Museum · City Hall · Natal Playhouse Theatre · ROYAL · Convent · ALBANY · RIVIERA · Da Gama Clock · Dick King Statue · Pleasure Cruises · Point Yacht Club · Royal Natal Yacht Club · Old House Museum · Esplanade Gardens · Boatmans · Canal · Maydon Wharf

Snake Park · John Mc Intyre · Minitown · Somtseu Road Pier · MINITOWN HOLIDAY INN GARDEN COURT NORTH BEACH · Amphitheatre · Pavilion · Exhibition Hall · Playfair · Playfair · HOLIDAY INN CROWNE PLAZA · Beachfront · North Beach · Marine Drive · North Beach Pier · Parking · Parade · HOLIDAY INN GARDEN COURT MARINE PARADE · PROTEA EDWARD · Funworld · THE BALMORAL · FOUR SEASONS · PALM BEACH · TROPICANA · PROTEA SEABOARD · HOLIDAY INN GARDEN COURT SOUTH BEACH · Trampolines · Little Top Theatre · The Wheel Shopping Complex · OCEAN WALK · Addington · Point Clinic · Masonic · Addington Children's · Ripley · uShaka Marine World · Addington Primary School

BERKELEY · KE Masinga · Sylvester Ntuli · John Milne · Victoria Park · Samora Machel · Anton Lembede · TUDOR HOUSE · Cato · Statue · Department of Customs and Excise · Maritime Museum · BAT Centre · Quayside · Ocean Terminal and T Jetty · Bay of Natal · Shepstone · South Beach Ave

INDIAN OCEAN · Bay of Plenty · Bay of Plenty Pier · North Beach

Scale 1 : 23 000
0 — 250 — 500 m
0 — 250 — 500 yd
N

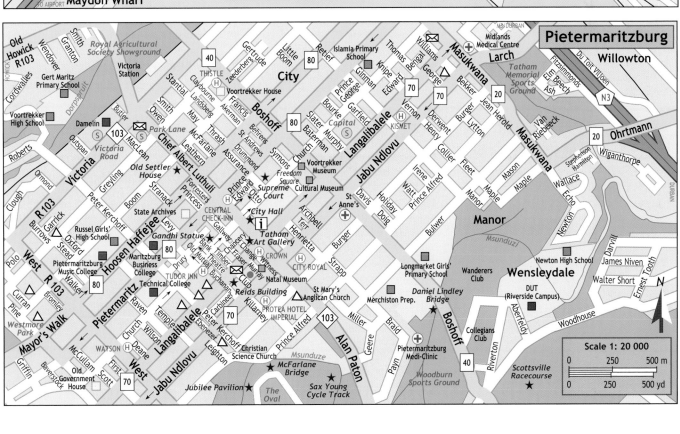

Pietermaritzburg

Old Howick R103 · Royal Agricultural Society Showground · Victoria Station · Gert Maritz Primary School · Voortrekker High School · Damelin · Park Lane · Victoria Road · Old Settler House · Russel Girls' High School · Pietermaritzburg Music College · Maritzburg Business College · Pietermaritzburg Technical College · Westmore Park · Mayor's Walk · Old Government House

THISTLE · City · Little Boom · Retief · Islamia Primary School · Thomas Knipe · Williams · Masukwana · Midlands Medical Centre · Larch · Willowton · Tatham Memorial Sports Ground · N3 · Ohrtmann · Wiganthorpe · DURBAN

Boshoff · Voortrekker House · Freedom Square · Voortrekker Museum · Cultural Museum · Supreme Court · St Anne's · KISMET · Capital · Langalibalele · Jabu Ndlovu · Manor · Msunduzi · Wensleydale · Wanderers Club · Newton High School · James Niven · Walter Short

Central Check-Inn · Gandhi Statue · Tatham Art Gallery · City Hall · CROWN · Witness · CITY ROYAL · Natal Museum · St Mary's Anglican Church · Merchiston Prep. · Longmarket Girls' Primary School · Daniel Lindley Bridge · DUT (Riverside Campus) · Collegians Club · Scottsville Racecourse

Christian Science Church · McFarlane Bridge · Jubilee Pavilion · The Oval · Sax Young Cycle Track · PROTEA HOTEL IMPERIAL · Woodburn Sports Ground · Pietermaritzburg Medi-Clinic · Manor · Wensleydale

Scale 1 : 20 000
0 — 250 — 500 m
0 — 250 — 500 yd
N

KwaZulu-Natal Drakensberg

South Africa's highest mountain range, the Drakensberg is a massive and strikingly beautiful rampart of deep gorges, pinnacles and saw-edged ridges, caves, overhangs and balancing rocks. In the winter months its upper levels lie deep in snow, but clustered among the foothills far below, in undulating grassland, is a score of resort hotels established and run for the most part for family holiday-makers. People come for the fresh, clean mountain air; for the walks, climbs and drives; for the gentler sports (trout fishing, golf, bowls and horseback riding); and for casual relaxation in the most exquisite surrounds.

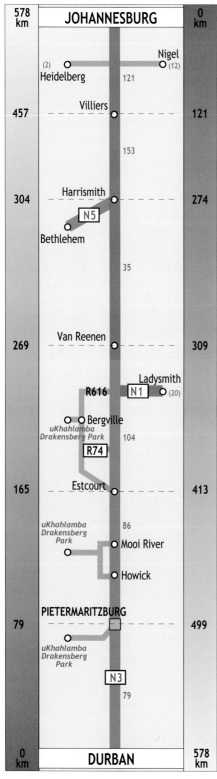

ACCOMMODATION

Cathedral Peak Hotel, Winterton, tel: 036 488 1888, fax: 488 1889; set amid spectacular peaks.
Drakensberg Sun Lifestyle Resort, Winterton, tel: 036 468 1000, fax: 468 1224; wonderful views.
Little Switzerland Hotel, between Bergville and Harrismith, tel: 036 438 2500, fax: 438 2517; view of the spectacular Amphitheatre.

Sani Pass Hotel, Himeville, tel: 033 702 1320, fax: 702 0220; 800ha (1977 acres) situated at the foot of Sani Pass.
Champagne Castle Hotel, tel: 036 468 1063, fax: 468 1306; guided walks; golf course.
Orion Mont-Aux-Sources Hotel, tel: 036 438 8000; 7km (4.3 miles) from the Royal Natal National Park.

MAIN ATTRACTIONS

Royal Natal National Park: an extensive and beautiful floral and wildlife sanctuary. Excursions to the Mont-Aux-Sources plateau and the spectacular uThukela Falls, the country's highest waterfall.
Champagne Castle: a magnificent peak and one of the Drakensberg's easier climbs.
Giant's Castle Game Reserve: in the central Drakensberg, a scenic wonderland famous for its Bushman (San) rock art and raptor conservation programmes.
Ndedema Gorge: 'place of rolling thunder'; a magnificent gorge renowned for its rock art.
Himeville Nature Reserve: in the southern Drakensberg; a paradise for trout fishermen.
The Midlands Meander: a scenic route takes travellers through Meander outlets and picturesque villages. See art and craft studios, herb and flower farms, country pubs, breweries, and much more!

USEFUL CONTACTS

Drakensberg Tourism Association, near Bergville, tel: 036 448 1557.
Central Drakensberg Information Centre, tel: 036 488 1207.
Mountain Club of SA, (KZN section) tel: 031 260 1077.
Drakensberg Boys Choir School, tel: 036 468 1012, except during school holidays.
Midlands Meander Tourism, for information tel: 033 330 8195; website: www.midlandsmeander.co.za

Right: *The impressive Giant's Castle, formed by vast lava outpourings of the Drakensberg Basalt Formation (to a thickness of more than 1000m) is just one of the formations to be found in the beautiful Drakensberg mountain range.*

Drakensberg

Free State

Scale 1: 800 000

Phuthaditjhaba
Bushman Paintings
Babangiboni 2329 m ▲
Hlolela 2188 m ▲
Witsieshoek Mountain Resort
LITTLE SWITZERLAND
Olviershoek
The Cavern Berg Resort
Hlalanathi Berg Resort
ROYAL NATAL
ORION
MONT-AUX-SOURCES
uThukela Falls
3282 m Mont-Aux-Sources
Tendele
Royal Natal National Park (World Heritage Site)
Sterkfontein Dam
Sterkfontein Dam NR
Kerkenberg ★
Kilburn Dam
Woodstock Dam
Driel Dam
Tevreden Cheese Farm

Swinburne
Oban Guest Farm
De Beers Pass
Van Reenen
1944 m
Smallest Church in South Africa
Van Reenen's
Wyford
Brakwal
Lions Rump
ANDREW
Bethlehem/Kestell
WARDEN

Geluksburg
Sand River Valley
Besters
Smith's Crossing
Pepworth
Colworth
Matiwane
Elandslaagte
Elandslaagte
Doornkraal
Himeville Bridge
NEWCASTLE

Quedusizi Dam
PROTEA CROWN
Ladysmith
Rensburg
Lombardskop
Wagon Hill
Umbulwana
Pieters
Little Niagra Falls
Roosboom
Ambleside Military Cemetery
Clauston Field of Remembrance
Colenso
Pieter's Hill
Toll House and Bulwer Bridge
BATTLEFIELDS
Chieveley Train Disaster
Chieveley
Bloukrans Monument
Old Mill & Voortrekker House
Weenen
Weenen GR

DRAKENSBERG

Rock Paintings
Cathedral Peak ▲ 3004 m
Cleft Peak 3280 m
Mlambonja Wilderness Area
CATHEDRAL PEAK
Mike's Pass
Meteorological Station
DRAKENSBERG SUN LIFESTYLE RESORT
THE NEST
Ndedema Gorge
Cathkin Peak 3148 m
Champagne Castle 3246 m
Monk's Cowl
CHAMPAGNE CASTLE
Dragon Peaks
Monk's Cowl Country Club
KwaZulu Weavers
Voortrekker Memorial
Loskop
Draycott
Winterton
BRIDGE
Zunckels
Zinckels

Source of Orange River
Mafadi 3446 m
Injasuti Hillside
Giant's Castle Game Reserve
Popple Peak 3330 m
Giant's Lodge
uKhahlamba Drakensberg Park (World Heritage Site)
Ntabamhlope White Mountain Resort
Rockmount
Highmoor Wilderness Area
Highmoor Dam
Motsitseng

LESOTHO

Mokhotlong
Sangebethu
Giant's Castle 3317 m
Loteni Nature Reserve
Kamberg
Kamberg NR
Redcliffe
Crane Foundation
Mt Lebanon 2126 m
Hlatikulu
Neljidwane
Soutar's Hill
Masenkeng
Thabana Ntlenyana 3482 m
Redi 3298 m
Vergelegen Nature Reserve
Ngcingweni Forest
Vergelegen
Gelib Tree Hiking Trail
Lower Loteni
Mkhomazi
Mkhomazi Wilderness Area
Pingpong Cutting
Loteni

Sani Pass
Sani
Hodgson's Peak 3257 m
uKhahlamba Drakensberg Park (World Heritage Site)
Thamatuwe 3431m
Garden Castle NR
Cobham NR
Cobham
DRAKENSBERG GARDEN
Bushman's Nek
BUSHMAN'S NEK
KINGSCOTE
HIMEVILLE ARMS
Old Prison Building
Himeville NR
Splashy Fen
Himeville
UNDERBERG INN
Underberg
Pevensey
The Swamp NR
Oribi Conservancy
MOUNTAIN PARK
Bulwer
DONNYBROOK

KwaZulu-Natal

Ennersdale
SUNRISE
PLOUGH
Estcourt
Zaailaager
Wagendrift NR
New Beacon Hill
Lowlands
Brynbella/Willow Grange
WILLOW GRANGE
Griffin's Hill
Hidcote
South Downs
SWISS MANOR
Mooi River
Rosetta
Nottingham Road
NOTTINGHAM ROAD
Nottingham
Balgowan
Umgeni Vlei NR
Lidgetton
Dargle
Mpendle 1967m
iMpendle
EVERGLADES
Boston
Devon
Deepdale
Elandskop
Taylors
Rensburg Koppies
Middelrus
The Grove
Craigie Burn NR
Craigie Burn Dam
Rietvlei
Karkloof NR
Curry's Post
Midlands Meander
Lions River
Karkloof Falls
Midmar NR
Midmar Dam
Howick
Howick Falls
Merrivale
Queen Elizabeth Park
Hilton
Albert Falls NR
Sweet Waters
PIETERMARITZBURG
Henley Dam
Edendale
NEW HANOVER
RICHMOND
GRETTOWN

Historic Battlefields

*F*or most of the 19th century, the KwaZulu-Natal battlefields region was a bloody battlefield, as Zulu, Boer and Briton fought for territorial supremacy. Military enthusiasts will find the Battlefields Route (which includes the sites of Blood River, iSandlwana, Rorke's Drift, uLundi, Majuba Hill, Talana, Elandslaagte, Tugela Heights, Colenso, Ladysmith and Spioenkop) fascinating. Some of the most dramatic confrontations occurred in the triangular area bounded by Estcourt in the south, Volksrust in the north, and Vryheid to the east.

THE BATTLEFIELDS ROUTE

Blood River (1838): the final and decisive clash between the Zulus and the Voortrekker settlers during the Boer migration into Natal. Raw courage proved no match for superior firepower — more than 3000 Zulus perished on the field; Boer losses amounted to just three wounded.

iSandlwana (1879): part of a British invading force was annihilated by a 24,000-strong *impi* (army); only a handful of the 1000-plus redcoats survived.

Rorke's Drift (1879): a bitterly fought skirmish in which a small British garrison held out against wave after wave of Zulu *impi*. Between them, the defenders earned 11 Victoria Crosses.

Majuba Hill (1881): final battle of the brief Anglo-Transvaal war, in which a Boer force of part-time soldiers drove the British regulars from the slopes of the high hill, inflicting severe casualties. The British commander, Sir George Colley, is thought to have committed suicide during the retreat.

Spioenkop (1900): the Anglo-Boer War's bloodiest battle, savagely fought between Boer and Briton for control of the strategic hill on the route leading to the besieged Ladysmith. Casualties were high on both sides; the Boers eventually prevailed.

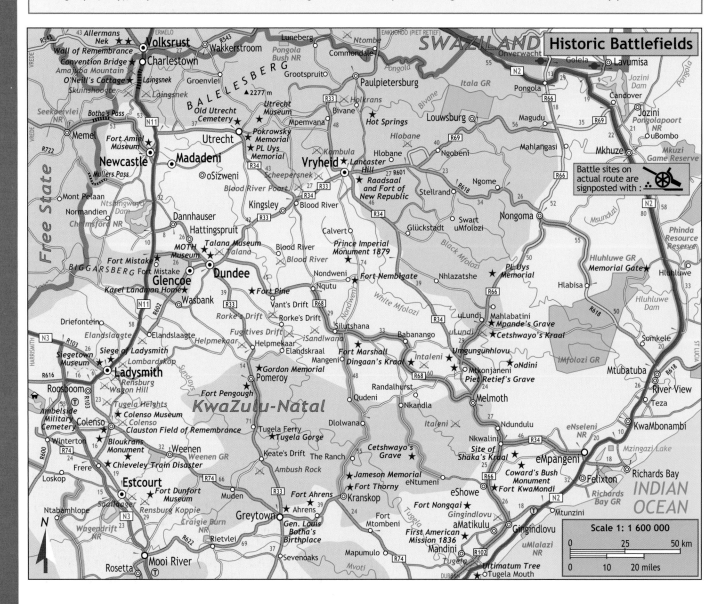

Wild Coast

Southwestwards from the KwaZulu-Natal border lies the Transkei region, its rugged seaboard known as the Wild Coast — an unspoilt and quite beautiful 280km (174-mile) long wilderness of beaches and secluded bays, lagoons and estuaries (an impressive 18 rivers find their way to the Indian Ocean along the coastal strip), imposing cliffs and rocky reefs that probe, finger-like, out to sea. Rolling green hills and patches of dense vegetation grace the hinterland. Largest of its seaside villages are Port St Johns and Coffee Bay; most prominent resort, the superb Wild Coast Sun.

TRAVEL TIPS

The N2 bisects this region, passing northeast to southwest from Port Shepstone through Kokstad, Mount Frere, Mthatha and Butterworth, where grocery supplies and petrol can be obtained. The gravel roads leading down to the coast can be rather taxing on both vehicle and driver. Beware of straying animals.

ACCOMMODATION

Wild Coast Sun, Transkei region, tel: 039 305 9111, fax: 305 2863; glitz and glamour.
Trennery's Hotel, tel: 047 498 0004, fax: 498 0011; beautifully situated on Great Kei River, Kentani district.

Above: *The strange detached cliff known as Hole-in-the-Wall is a well-known spot not far from Coffee Bay on the beautiful Wild Coast.*

MAIN ATTRACTIONS

Wild Coast Sun: an extravagant, luxury hotel-casino complex situated right on the beachfront.
Hole-in-the-Wall: a short drive south of Coffee Bay stands a massive detached cliff with a small arched opening through which the surf thunders.
Mazeppa Bay: palm trees line three wide beaches; the scuba diving, snorkelling and fishing spots are superb.
Qhorha Mouth: a good beach with interesting rock pools, close to the hotel. In the **Dwesa** and **Cwebe nature reserves** buffalo, eland and warthog roam the combined forest and grassland, while crocodiles patrol the rivers.
Fishing: catches range from kob, blacktail bronze bream and shad to barracuda and trophy-sized sharks.

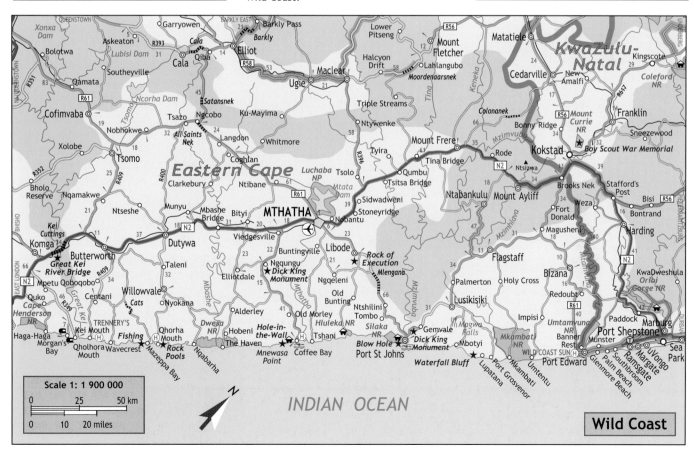

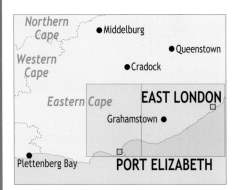

Eastern Cape

The region, extending from the KwaZulu-Natal border and the Wild Coast southwestward, through Algoa Bay, to the lush evergreen Tsitsikamma park, and inland to the foothills of the Drakensberg and the semi-arid edges of the Great Karoo, offers scenic diversity and splendour. The provincial capital is the small town of Bhisho, though Port Elizabeth serves as its economic centre.

ACCOMMODATION

Fish River
Tsolwana Nature Reserve, tel: 043 742 4450; three well-appointed homesteads.
Fish River Sun Hotel, tel: 040 676 1101; up-market resort.
Hogsback
Hogsback Inn, tel: 045 962 1006; beautiful nature walks and prolific bird life.

USEFUL CONTACTS

Nelson Mandela Bay Tourism, Port Elizabeth, tel: 041 585 8884.
Tourism Buffalo City, East London, tel: 043 722 6015, fax: 743 5091.
Grahamstown Tourism Information/Makana Tourism, tel: 046 622 3241, fax: 622 3266.
Automobile Association (AA), the nationwide AA emergency rescue service number is, tel: 083 843 22.

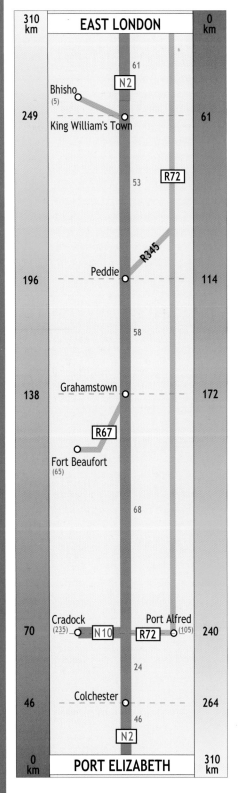

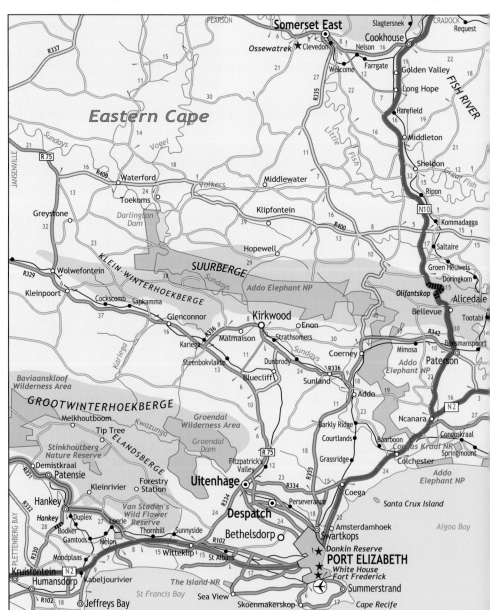

TRAVEL TIPS

The N2 leads west to Cape Town and northeast to Durban. The R32 links Port Elizabeth with Cradock. Wild Coast resorts are accessible via subsidiary (often gravel) roads leading off the N2. When using these roads, beware of potholes, hairpin bends and straying animals.

Right: *Grahamstown is known as the 'City of Saints' for the large number of its churches and as the 'settler city' for its British-colonial origins. For an insight into South African theatre, dance, music, film, fine arts and crafts, don't miss the National Festival of the Arts held in July every year.*

MAIN ATTRACTIONS

Jeffreys Bay: a surfer's paradise.
Grahamstown: academic and cultural centre; hosts acclaimed National Arts Festival each June/July.
Great Fish River Conservation Area: home to hippo, buffalo and black rhino.
Tsolwana Nature Reserve: truly magnificent mountain reserve.
Hogsback: northwest of King William's Town, set among the exquisite forests which provided the inspiration for JRR Tolkien's novel, *The Hobbit*.
Port Alfred: pretty resort town at the mouth of the Kowie River.
Shamwari Game Reserve: the southernmost private big game reserve in Africa — malaria free.

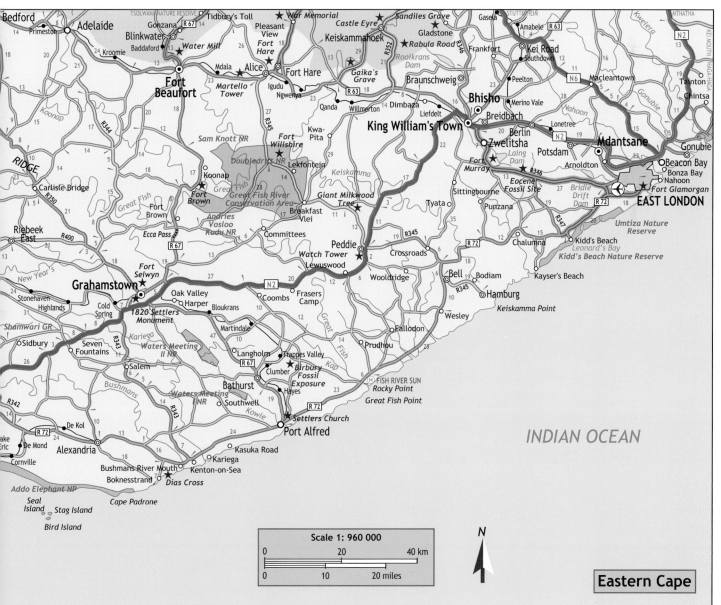

Scale 1: 960 000

Eastern Cape

Port Elizabeth

*K*nown as the 'friendly city' and also as the 'windy city', Port Elizabeth is the economic hub of the Eastern Cape, much of its industrial activity revolving around the vehicle assembly sector and related enterprises. P.E., as it is most often called, is also a major tourist centre. Set on the shores of Algoa Bay, the country's fifth largest metropolis has some excellent beaches, many historic buildings, sophisticated shopping centres, good hotels and restaurants. Port Elizabeth owes its origins to the 4000 British settlers who landed here in 1820.

MAIN ATTRACTIONS

Beaches: Port Elizabeth has four major beaches: King's, Humewood, Hobie and Pollok, each with its special attractions.

Bayworld and Museum Complex: at Humewood; see the performing dolphins and seals and visit the Aquarium and Snake Park.

Nature rambles: in and around P.E. lie **St Georges Park** and the **Pearson Conservatory**, **Settlers Park**, the **Island Conservation Area** and the beautifully tended **Van Stadens Wild Flower Reserve**.

Addo Elephant National Park: this park, located about 72km (45 miles) northeast of the city, was created in 1931 to protect the few remaining survivors of the once-prolific herds of Cape elephant. The sanctuary offers good game-viewing and comfortable accommodation.

Donkin Heritage Trail: a steeply winding historical walking tour.

Fort Frederick: building of historical significance built in 1799; located on Belmont Terrace, overlooking the Baakens River estuary.

Sardinia Bay: marine reserve with miles of unspoilt coastline and crystal clear water; excellent for diving, horse riding and scenic walks or hikes.

Boardwalk Casino and Entertainment World: family entertainment, shopping, dining and gaming; set around a series of man-made lakes and beautiful gardens lit by 40,000 Tivoli lights.

ACCOMMODATION

Beach Hotel, Humewood, tel: 041 583 2161, fax: 583 6220; close to Bayworld and Hobie Beach.

The Edward Hotel, tel: 041 586 2056, fax: 586 4925; Edwardian-style; overlooks Donkin Memorial.

The Humewood Hotel, Beach Road, tel: 041 585 8961, fax: 585 1740; family hotel, attractive rooms.

Formula 1 Hotel, Beach Road, tel: 041 585 6380, fax: 585 6383; budget.

Protea Lodge, Prospect Hill, tel/fax: 041 585 1721; budget, Victorian comfort, self-catering.

King's Tide Boutique Hotel: tel: 041 583 6023, fax: 041 583 3389; central reservation tel: 086 111 5720; four-star luxury, indoor/outdoor entertainment.

USEFUL CONTACTS

St George's Hospital, tel: 041 392 6111, fax: 392 6000.

Automobile Association, emergency number, tel: 083 843 22.

Computicket, tel: 083 915 8000.

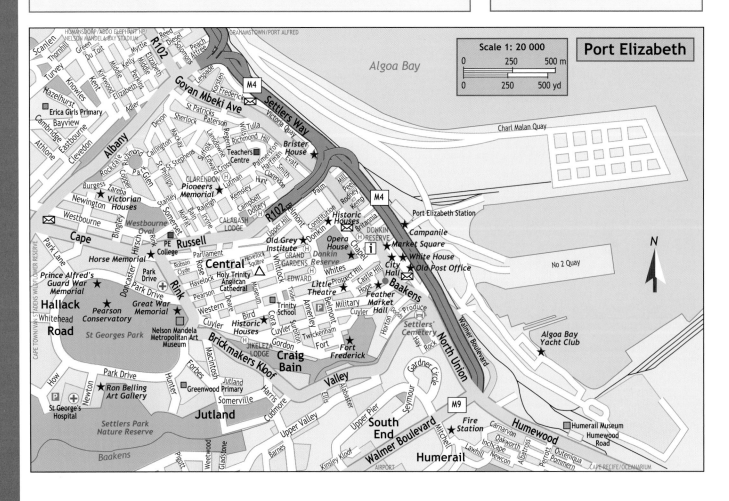

East London

*S*ituated at the mouth of the Buffalo River, the river port of East London combines the charm of a relatively small community with all the essential amenities of a large city. Its attractions are of the quiet, undemanding, family-orientated kind: it has fine beaches, pleasant parks and gardens, good hotels and restaurants, and some entertaining nightlife in the summer months, especially in the seafront area. The principal thoroughfare, Oxford Street, is lined with a variety of modern shops, many of which cater to the tourist trade. The port serves the industries of the Eastern Cape and the Free State.

MAIN ATTRACTIONS

Superb beaches: most popular and accessible is Orient Beach.
East London Museum: Oxford Street; exhibits include the first coelacanth (hitherto thought to be extinct) to be caught and the world's only dodo egg.
Aquarium: over 400 species.
Queens Park Botanical Gardens: splendour of indigenous flora.
Ann Bryant Gallery: fine local paintings and sculptures.
Hiking trails: a choice of walks from the 4-day Shipwreck Trail to the two-hour Umtiza Trail lead nature lovers along unspoilt beaches, through nature reserves, or into the Amatola mountains to the northwest of East London.
Latimer's Landing: a waterfront development on the banks of the Buffalo River. It offers a variety of restaurants overlooking the small craft anchorage where various boat and yacht rides are offered.

ACCOMMODATION

Blue Lagoon Hotel, Blue Bend Place, Beacon Bay, tel: 043 748 4821, fax: 748 2037; situated very close to the beach.
Dolphin View Lodge, Seaview Terrace, tel: 043 702 8600. On the beachfront.
Garden Court East London, cnr John Bailey and Moore streets, tel: 043 722 7260, fax: 743 7360; on beachfront, standard rooms, service and value.
Kennaway Protea, tel: 043 722 5531; close to the city centre and the beaches, solid value.

Premier Hotel King David, cnr Currie Street and Inverleith Terrace, tel: 043 722 3174. Very central.
Windsor Cabanas and The Courtyard, tel: 043 743 2225; Mediterranean-style, fine views, self-catering option.
The Thatch Guest House, 37 Flamingo Crescent, Beacon Bay, tel: 043 748 3672, fax: 748 6227. Offers luxury and tranquility. Close to the city centre.
Tidewaters B&B, 1 Tidewaters Drive, Gonubie, tel: 043 740 4505, fax: 740 5813; on Gonubie River, with spa.

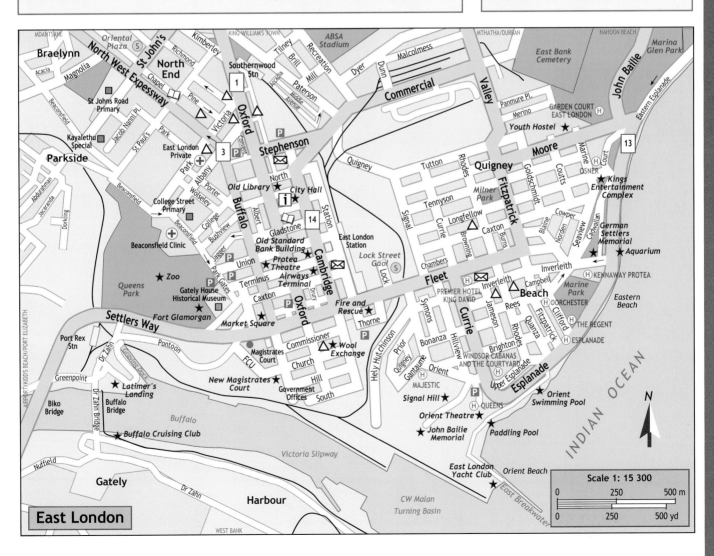

East London

Garden Route

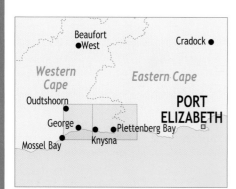

*T*he southern coastal terrace, extending from Humansdorp, the Tsitsikamma and Storms River in the east to Mossel Bay and beyond in the west, is known as the Garden Route. This is an enchanting shoreline of lovely bays and coves, high cliffs and wide estuaries, with a hinterland of mountains, spectacular passes, rivers, waterfalls and wooded ravines. The lagoons and lakes around Knysna and Wilderness are magical stretches of water. The attractions are many: good hotels and eating places, pleasant villages and resorts, and a warm ocean that beckons bather, yachtsman and angler alike. Inland you'll find the town of Oudtshoorn, its surrounding ostrich farms and, to the north, the magnificent Cango Caves.

ACCOMMODATION

Wilderness
Protea Hotel Wilderness,
tel: 044 877 1110, fax: 877 0600; excellent quality, set between forest and sea. Conference facilities available.
Fairy Knowe Hotel,
tel: 044 877 1100, fax: 877 0364; on the banks of the Touws River.
Wilderness Beach Hotel,
tel: 044 877 1104. Overlooks the ocean.
Knysna
Brenton-on-Sea,
tel: 044 381 0081; 15km (9 miles) from Knysna.

Plettenberg Bay
Beacon Island Lifestyle Resort,
tel: 044 533 1120, fax: 533 3880; smart, in a unique setting.
Tsala Treetop Lodge,
tel: 044 532 7818; exclusive retreat.
Sedgefield
Lake Pleasant Living,
tel: 044 343 1985, fax: 343 2589; five-star hotel, superb facilities.
Oudtshoorn
Protea Hotel Riempie Estate,
tel: 044 272 6161, fax: 272 6772; close to Highgate Ostrich Farm.

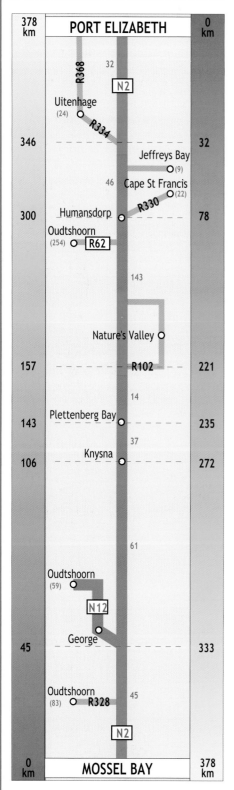

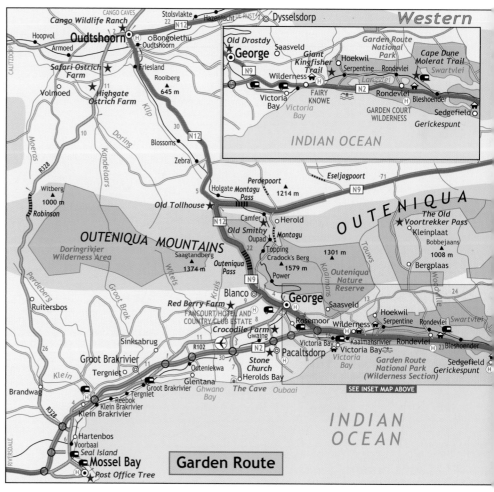

Garden Route

Below: Hikers on the Tsitsikamma Trail, which winds its way through the park's scenic countryside. Baboon, vervet monkey, honey badger and bushpig are often encountered.

MAIN ATTRACTIONS

Garden Route National Park (Tsitsikamma section) and **Otter Trail:** an 80km (50-mile) strip of superb coastline and large offshore marine reserve.
Storms River Mouth: dramatic scenery; spend a night in the chalets.
Plettenberg Bay: fashionable holiday resort with beautiful beaches.
Mossel Bay: excellent beaches and the Bartolomeu Dias Museum.
Goukamma Nature Reserve: short distance west of Knysna; unspoilt nature and wonderful bird life.

Garden of Eden: a beautiful forest area; many of its trees are labelled.
Knysna: charming little resort town with an attractive lagoon.
Wilderness Lake Area: superb scenery and prolific bird life.
Oudtshoorn: fascinating ostrich farms.
Cango Caves: complex of caverns ranked among the most remarkable of Africa's many natural wonders.
Bungi jumping: jump off Gourits River bridge or Bloukrans bridge. *See* www.faceadrenalin.com for more info.

USEFUL CONTACTS

Garden Route National Park Wilderness Section, tel: 044 877 0046, fax: 877 0366; **Tsitsikamma Section**, tel: 042 281 1607, fax: 281 1629.
Oudtshoorn Tourism Bureau, tel: 044 272 0041.
Mossel Bay Tourism Bureau, tel: 044 691 2202.

Plettenberg Bay Info, tel: 044 533 4065.
Wilderness Tourism, tel: 044 877 0045.
George Tourism Bureau, tel: 044 801 9299.
Knysna Private Hospital, tel: 044 384 1083.
Knysna Tourism, tel: 044 382 5510.

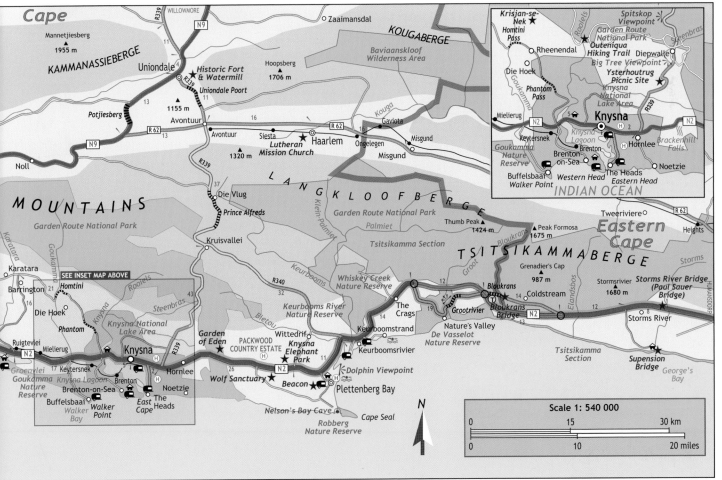

George

*T*his pleasant little city, which was named after England's King George III, lies at the foot of the splendid Outeniqua Mountains and is the Garden Route's principal urban centre. The surrounding countryside is given over to mixed farming, forestry and the cultivation of hops. The town is linked to Knysna by the main Garden Route highway.

MAIN ATTRACTIONS

Outeniqua Choo-Tjoe: board this old steam train for a museum-to-museum trip to Mossel Bay. This 52km (32-mile) journey offers beautiful views of the Garden Route; tel: 044 801 8288.
George Museum: in the Old Drostdy; noted for its antique musical instruments.
Churches: visit St Mark's, South Africa's smallest cathedral; the Dutch Reformed church, completed in 1842; and St Peter and St Paul, the oldest Roman Catholic church in the country.
Beaches: excellent bathing, fishing and sun-worshipping at Herold's and Victoria bays.

Above: *The Outeniqua Choo-Tjoe, an old steam train, offers tourists an especially scenic excursion between George and Mossel Bay.*

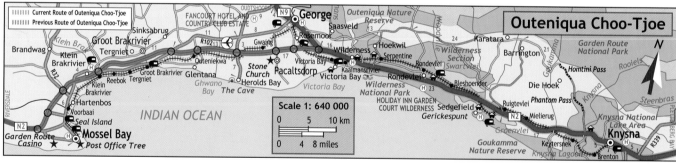

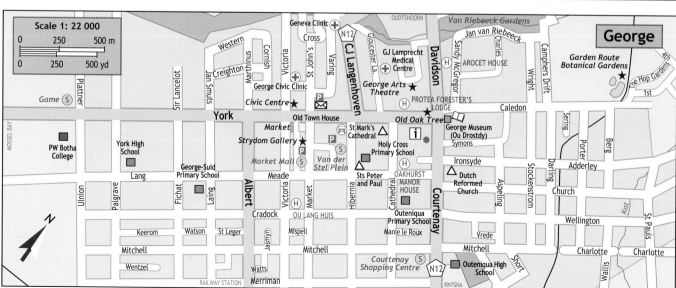

Knysna

*K*nysna is one of the Garden Route's best-known travel destinations. Nature quite literally knocks on your front door. The town nestles on the shores of an estuary fed by rivers originating in the Outeniqua Mountains, it is surrounded by lush indigenous forests and is cooled by a sea breeze from the Indian Ocean. In and around Knysna one will find a selection of fine restaurants (the famous Knysna oyster features on many a menu), activities, cultural and heritage experiences, adventure and natural encounters to match your mood, age, physique and budget. For the shopper there are interesting outlets around every corner, including a quaint Waterfront shopping complex and authentic African traders.

MAIN ATTRACTIONS

Knysna Heads: two promontories guarding the entrance to Knysna Lagoon, with good views of the surrounds.
Royal Hotel: Prince Alfred and George Bernard Shaw stayed here.
Millwood Museum: local history, gold mining and timber industry.
Fresh oysters: try some, sprinkled with fresh lemon juice or hot chilli sauce, at the Knysna Oyster Co.
Crab's Creek: a restaurant on the water's edge; sit under umbrellas and enjoy the prolific bird life.
Noetzie: stroll past the five castles overlooking the sea (please note that they are private residences).
Knysna Forest: together with the Tsitsikamma Forest, it forms the largest expanse of indigenous high forest in South Africa.
Knysna Elephant Park: educates all ages about the Knysna elephants, tel: 044 532 7732, fax: 532 7763.
Featherbed Nature Reserve, ferry ride across the bay to the lovely reserve where you can hike, picnic, or dine at the restaurant, tel: 044 382 1693, fax: 382 2373.

ACCOMMODATION

Belvidere Manor, tel: 044 387 1055; historic home at the edge of the lagoon.
Point Lodge, tel: 044 382 1944; lakeside, owner-managed, friendly, tranquil setting, *en-suite* rooms.
Leisure Isle Lodge, on Ballard Bay, tel: 044 384 0462; top-rated guesthouse, superb views.
Yellowwood Lodge, tel: 044 382 5906; owner-managed, friendly, beautiful *en-suite* rooms, fine views of lagoon.
Inyathi Guest Lodges, tel: 044 382 7768, e-mail: info@inyathiguestlodge.co.za Individually decorated wooden chalets in the heart of Knysna set in a mostly indigenous garden. Multilingual owner.

The Russell Hotel, cnr Long, Unity and Graham sts, tel: 044 382 1058; luxurious hotel centrally situated within walking distance of all Knysna's popular attractions.
Pezula Resort Hotel, Lagoonview Drive, Pezula Estate, tel: 044 302 3410 (reservations); exclusive cliff-top retreat with its own golf course.
Lightleys Holiday Houseboats, Belvidere Off-ramp, Phantom Pass Road, N2, Belvidere/Brenton, tel: 044 386 0007; catered or self-catered, fully equipped 2-, 4- and 6-berth boats on the safe, tranquil waters of the Knysna Lagoon. Ideal for family holidays or romantic getaways.

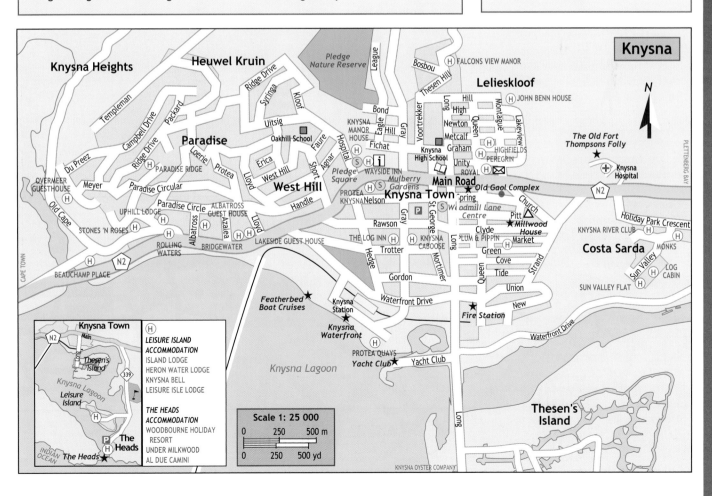

Cape Winelands

To the north and east of Cape Town is the Winelands, a region of grand mountain ranges, fertile valleys, vineyards and orchards, and of homesteads built in the distinctive and gracious Cape Dutch style. Among its more notable attractions are the various wine routes. Stellenbosch, the country's second oldest urban centre, is the principal town.

MAIN ATTRACTIONS

Stellenbosch: hub of the wineland region; a picturesque university town that prides itself on its lovely historic buildings and oak-lined avenues.

Franschhoek: founded by French Huguenots between 1680 and 1690. Protestant settlers were forbidden to form independent communities and, through intermarriage, lost much of their cultural heritage, but they left an indelible mark on the local wine-growing industry.

Paarl: original farming settlement established in 1720; visit a number of splendid wine estates in the vicinity of this little town.

Somerset West: the beautiful big homestead of Vergelegen estate was built by an early Cape governor and completed in 1701.

Durbanville: situated in peaceful surroundings, the wine estates offer high-quality wines.

USEFUL CONTACTS

Durbanville Tourism Office, tel: 021 970 3172.

Vignerons de Franschhoek (Wine Route), tel: 021 876 2861.

Franschhoek Tourism Bureau, tel: 021 876 3603, fax: 876 2964.

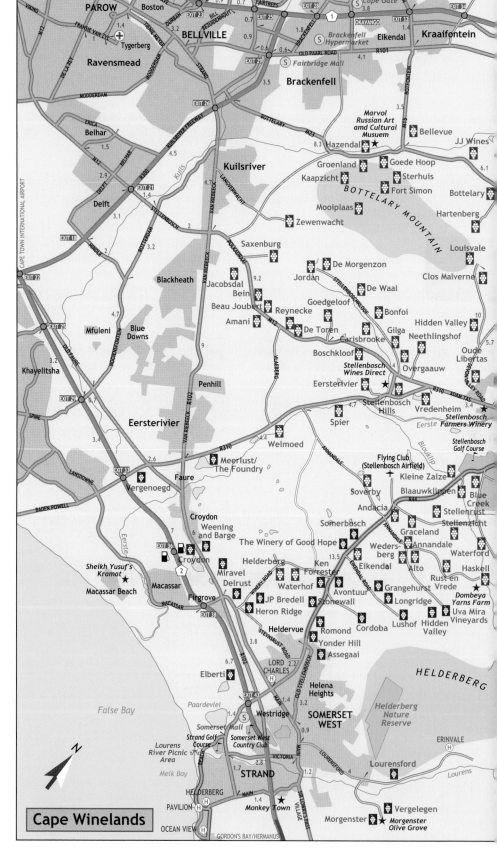

Cape Winelands

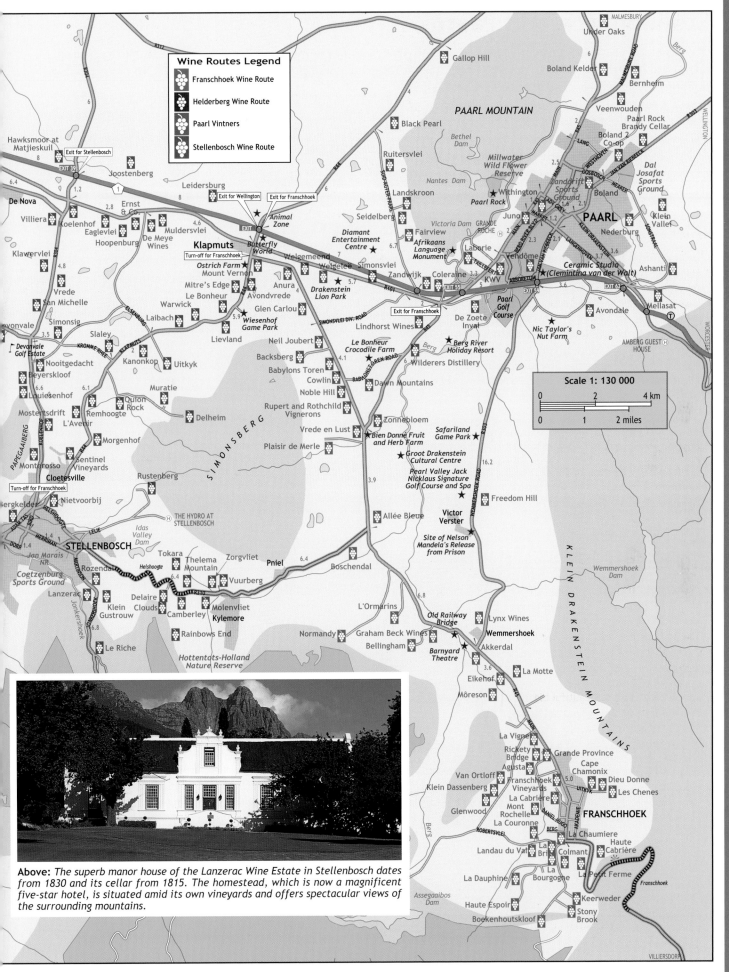

Above: *The superb manor house of the Lanzerac Wine Estate in Stellenbosch dates from 1830 and its cellar from 1815. The homestead, which is now a magnificent five-star hotel, is situated amid its own vineyards and offers spectacular views of the surrounding mountains.*

Stellenbosch and Paarl

Stellenbosch, South Africa's second oldest urban centre and heart of the Winelands lies in a pleasant valley, less than an hour's drive from Cape Town. Founded in 1669, the settlement matured gracefully over the centuries, its broad thoroughfares lined by stately oaks and splendid historic buildings. It is the hub of an enchanting wine route and a leading seat of learning, home to a major university and several respected schools. Paarl, the biggest of the region's towns, began in 1720 as a farming and wagon-building centre, taking its name from the pearl-like cluster of granite rocks atop the overlooking mountain.

ACCOMMODATION

Grande Roche Hotel, Plantasie Street, Paarl, tel: 021 863 2727; elegant hotel with award-winning Bosman's Restaurant.

Lanzerac Manor and Winery, Lanzerac Road, Stellenbosch, tel: 021 887 1132; superb facilities, elegantly refurbished; wine made on the premises.

D'Ouwe Werf, 30 Church Street, Stellenbosch, tel: 021 887 4608; tradition and atmosphere combined.

L'Auberge Rozendal, Omega Road, Jonkershoek, tel: 021 809 2600; on a working wine farm.

USEFUL CONTACTS

Stellenbosch Wine Route Office, tel: 021 886 4310.
Stellenbosch Tourism and Information Bureau, tel: 021 883 3584, fax: 883 8017.
Paarl Vintners, tel: 021 863 4886.
Paarl Tourism Bureau, tel: 021 872 0860.

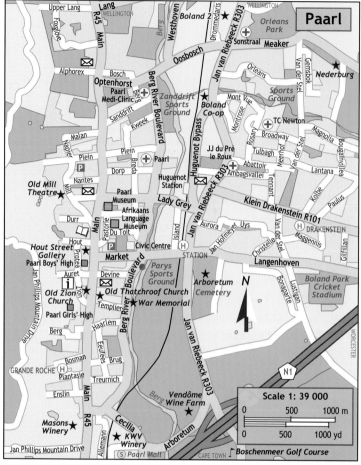

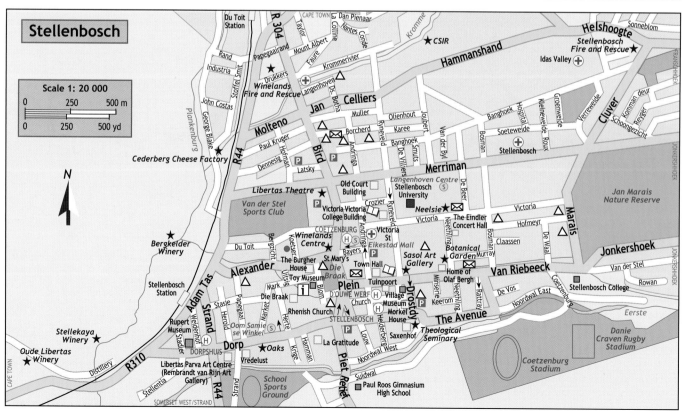

West Coast

The western shores of the country, pounded by the cold Atlantic Ocean, are a rather barren region of low coastal vegetation. Sleepy fishing villages bake in the sun, while inland small farming communities huddle together in the vast emptiness. But the area is transformed after the spring rains, when a carpet of flowers erupts in a riot of colour stretching as far as the eye can see.

MAIN ATTRACTIONS

West Coast National Park: beautiful natural wetland reserve with prolific **bird life** and magnificent wild flowers each spring (August–October).
Langebaan Lagoon: a 16km-long (10-mile) inlet, the focal point of the park and a paradise for bird-watchers, anglers, and water-sports enthusiasts.
Club Mykonos, a splendid Greek-style leisure and accommodation complex, is located nearby.

Above: *After the spring rains, the parched land lies resplendent in a colourful tapestry of flowers.*

ACCOMMODATION

Protea Hotel Saldanha Bay, 51B Main Street, Saldanha, tel: 022 714 1264, fax: 714 4093.
Lambert's Bay Hotel, 72 Voortrekker Street, Lambert's Bay, tel: 027 432 1126, fax: 432 1036; a comfortable and friendly establishment.

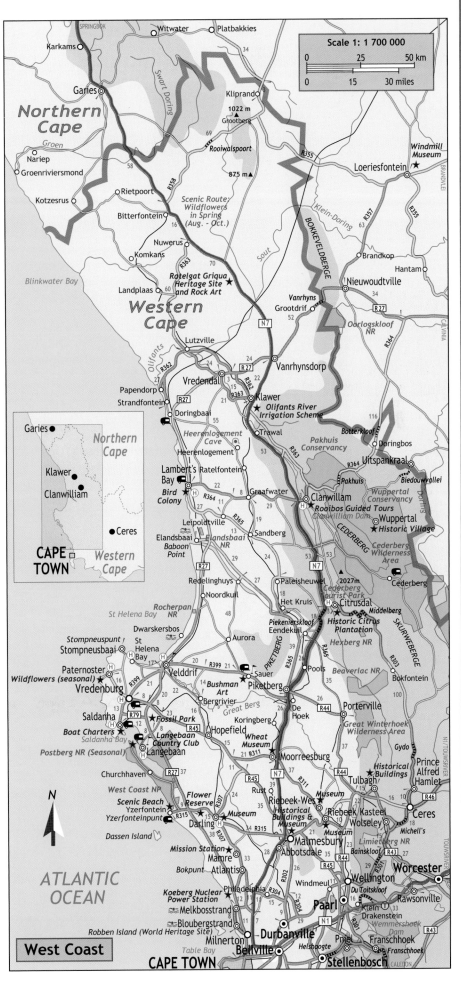

Scale 1: 1 700 000

West Coast

Western Cape

Ceres •

CAPE TOWN

• Paarl
• Stellenbosch

Caledon •

Cape Peninsula

The Cape Peninsula stretches from the Cape of Good Hope and Cape Point northward to Table Bay and comprises, for the most part, a strikingly beautiful plateau that achieves its loftiest and most spectacular heights in the famed Table Mountain massif overlooking Table Bay and Cape Town — a neat, bustling metropolis of handsome buildings, elegant thoroughfares and glittering shops. The Peninsula's western seaboard is scenically superb, its eastern shoreline graced by excellent beaches and attractive residential and resort centres that are a magnet for holiday-makers, scuba divers, boating enthusiasts, surfers and sun-worshippers.

Route map

258 km	LAINGSBURG	0 km
	Montagu ○ (84) R318	
102		
156	N1	102
	52	
	Worcester ○ (2) N15	
104		152
	Wolseley (42) ○ R43 14	
	Rawsonville ○ (3)	
90		168
	Wellington (20) ○ 30	
	R45 Franschhoek ○ (25)	
	Paarl ○ R45	
60		198
	12 Stellenbosch ○ (14)	
	R44	
48	R44 R101	208
	(16) ○ R304 Wellington 48	
	N1	
0 km	CAPE TOWN	258 km

ACCOMMODATION

Protea Hotel Sea Point, tel: 021 434 3344, fax: 434 3597; comfortable accommodation.
Peninsula All-Suite Hotel, Sea Point, tel: 021 430 7777, fax: 430 7776; on the promenade.
Alphen Hotel, tel: 021 794 5011, fax: 794 5710; charming wine estate in Constantia Valley.
Southern Sun Newlands Hotel, tel: 021 683 6562, fax: 683 6317; close to the Newlands cricket ground and rugby stadium.
The Vineyard Hotel, Newlands, tel: 021 657 4500, fax: 657 4501; historic country house.
The Lord Nelson Inn, Simon's Town, tel: 021 786 1386, fax: 786 1009; colonial-style inn offering old-fashioned hospitality.
Simon's Town Quayside Hotel, tel: 021 786 3838, fax: 786 2241; luxury hotel, waterfront setting.
Lord Charles Hotel, Somerset West, tel: 021 855 1040, fax: 855 1107; gracious elegance; world-class.

TRAVEL TIPS

Rail, bus and taxi services are adequate. Major international car-hire companies are represented, as are local car, camper, and caravan-hire firms. Tour operators offer a wide choice of one-day and half-day scenic coach trips. Please note: metered taxis must be booked or boarded at the designated stands, as they do not cruise for fares.

Above: *A cable car takes visitors up to the lookout at Cape Point for panoramic views of False Bay and the southern Atlantic Ocean.*

MAIN ATTRACTIONS

Cape Town: this charming metropolis is set beneath the majesty of Table Mountain. *See page 49.*
Table Mountain: *see page 49.*
Kirstenbosch: *see page 48.*
The V&A Waterfront: *see page 52.*
Chapman's Peak Drive: a world-renowned scenic route.
Clifton: chic suburb noted for its four magnificent beaches; popular with the trendier set.
Hout Bay: enchanting little suburb with a quaint fishing harbour.
Cape Point: southernmost tip of the Peninsula; the finest of view sites.
Robben Island: *see page 53.*
Simon's Town: the headquarters of the South African Navy, noted for its proximity to the fine beaches of Seaforth, as well as the African penguin colony at Boulders. For details, see www.simonstown.com
Constantia Wine Estates: five estates in the Constantia Valley: Groot and Klein Constantia, Buitenverwachting, Steenberg and Uitsig. Contact Groot Constantia for information, tel: 021 794 5128; fax: 794 1999.
Ratanga Junction: Africa's first full-scale theme park; family entertainment, tel: 0861 200 300.
GrandWest Casino: situated in Goodwood, includes gaming rooms, eateries and an olympic-size ice-rink, tel: 021 505 7777, fax: 534 1277.

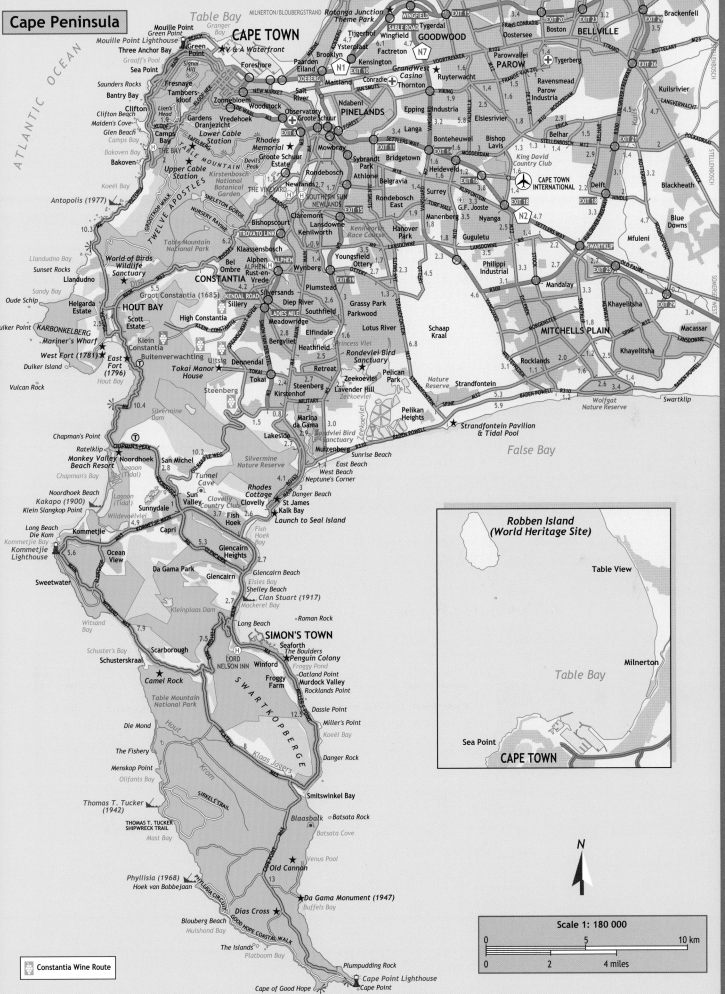

Cape Peninsula

Constantia Wine Route

Kirstenbosch

*T*he Kirstenbosch National Botanical Garden lies on the eastern slopes of the Table Mountain range. An astonishing array of flowering plants, representative of about a quarter of South Africa's 24,000 species, is cultivated here. Delightful walks lead through herb and fragrance gardens, and through stinkwood and yellowwood groves. There is a pelargonium koppie and a cycad amphitheatre, and the bird life, particularly the sunbirds drawn to the wealth of proteaceae, is enchanting. The Botanical Society Conservatory enables Kirstenbosch to display South African plants which cannot be grown in the outdoor gardens.

Above: *The rugged east face of the Table Mountain massif frames the delicate beauty of Kirstenbosch.*

ENCHANTED GARDEN

Fragrance garden: features plants with interesting scents and textures.
Visitors' Centre, tel: 021 799 8783. A glass conservatory and relaxing restaurant.
Van Riebeeck's hedge: part of the original wild almond hedge planted by the first Dutch settlers centuries ago.
The Dell: the oldest part of the garden; tree ferns and shade-loving plants.
Sunday music concerts: sundowner picnics in summer.
Kirstenbosch Garden, tel: 021 799 8899, www.sanbi.org

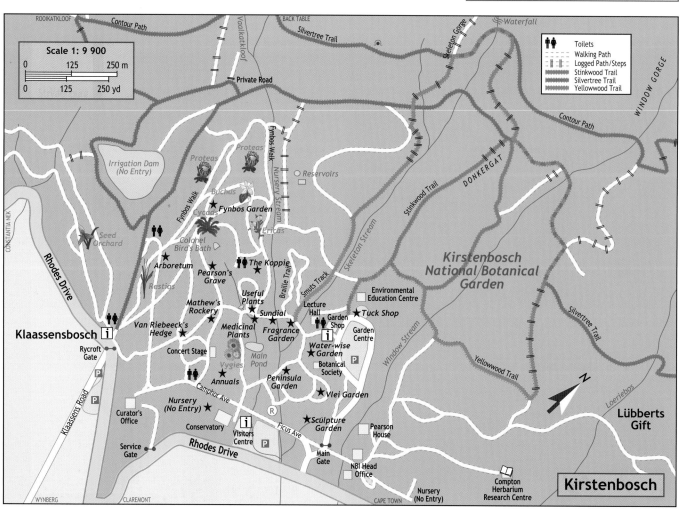

Cape Town

*T*he central metropolitan area of Cape Town huddles in a 'bowl' formed by Table Mountain, its flanking peaks and the broad sweep of Table Bay. Founded by Dutch settlers in 1652, this is the country's oldest city and fourth largest in terms of population. More than 300 years of history have created its unique architectural character — a vibrant blend of Dutch, French, English and Malay influences. It is an attractive, colourful city that boasts excellent hotels and restaurants, open-air markets and shops catering for every pocket and taste. The central area is small, compact, and easily explored on foot.

MAIN ATTRACTIONS

Table Mountain: ride the cable car or hike to the summit, and enjoy the breathtaking views.

Castle of Good Hope: the city's most notable edifice (built between 1666 and 1679).

Victoria and Alfred Waterfront: *see* page 52.

St George's Cathedral: visit the famous Rose Window over the south transept in this lovely church.

Greenmarket Square: for bargain hunting in one of Africa's prettiest little plazas. Be sure not to miss the **Old Town House** (built 1761) which contains the Michaelis collection of 17th-century Dutch and Flemish art, tel: 021 481 3933.

The Company Gardens: take a walk through the lush gardens founded by Jan van Riebeeck. While here, visit the South African Museum (tel: 021 481 3800), Planetarium and National Art Gallery.

Koopmans De Wet House: admire the beautiful antique furniture, tel: 021 481 3935.

Bargains: Cape Town's informal markets are the place to shop for contemporary African art, curios, ethnic jewellery and more. Try St George's Mall, Greenmarket Square and the Kirstenbosch Craft Market.

Rhodes Memorial: a grandiose monument with breathtaking views, located on the eastern slopes of Devil's Peak; lovely restaurant.

Signal Hill: have a sundowner and enjoy the panoramic view.

Bo-Kaap Museum: dedicated to the Malay culture; in one of the oldest original buildings, tel: 021 481 3939.

Cape Town Holocaust Centre: the only holocaust centre in Africa, tel: 021 462 5553, fax: 462 5554.

ACCOMMODATION

The Bunkhouse, 23 Antrim Road, Three Anchor Bay, tel/fax: 021 434 5695; budget accommodation.

The Cape Milner Hotel, 2a Milner Rodd, Tamboerskloof, tel: 021 426 1101, fax: 426 1109; conveniently close to town.

Cellars-Hohenort Hotel, Constantia, tel: 021 794 2137, fax: 794 2149; built 1693; lovely grounds; excellent restaurant.

Southern Sun Cullinan Hotel, Cullinan Street, tel: 021 415 4000, fax: 415 4051; central; excellent service.

Mount Nelson, Gardens, tel: 021 483 1000, fax: 483 1001; one of the world's most elegant hotels.

Southern Sun Cape Sun, Strand Street, tel: 021 488 5100, fax: 423 8875; centrel; excellent restaurants.

Park Inn, Greenmarket Square, tel: 021 423 2050, fax: 423 2059; charming position in the heart of town.

Protea President Hotel, Bantry Bay, tel: 021 434 8111, fax: 434 9991; luxurious, exquisitely sited on a rocky seafront.

Below: The arrival of the strong southeasterly wind is heralded by the appearance of the famous 'tablecloth' over Table Mountain.

EVENTS AND FESTIVALS

Minstrel Carnival: vibrant part of the **New Year** celebrations.

Metropolitan Handicap (J&B): horse-racing event held in **January**.

Cape Argus Pick 'n Pay Cycle Tour: held on the second **Sunday** of **March**.

Two Oceans Marathon: this popular event takes place on **Easter Saturday**.

Mother City Queer Project: annual gay/lesbian festival, held in **December**.

USEFUL CONTACTS

Cape Town Tourism, tel: 021 487 6800.

Groote Schuur Hospital, tel: 021 404 9111.

Table Mountain Aerial Cableway Co. Ltd, tel: 021 424 8181.

Castle of Good Hope, tel: 021 787 1249, fax: 787 1089.

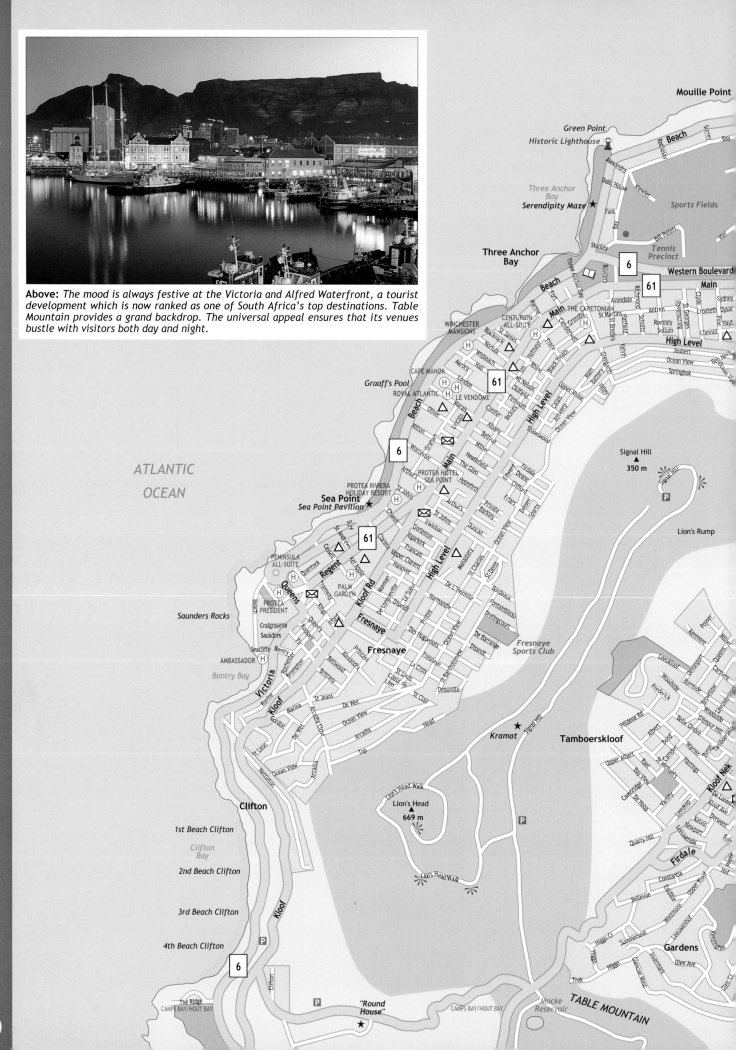

Above: *The mood is always festive at the Victoria and Alfred Waterfront, a tourist development which is now ranked as one of South Africa's top destinations. Table Mountain provides a grand backdrop. The universal appeal ensures that its venues bustle with visitors both day and night.*

V & A Waterfront

After a long separation, city and harbour are once again happily reunited through the ambitious Victoria and Alfred Waterfront redevelopment scheme, a multi-billion-rand private venture that borrowed ideas from the successful harbour projects of New York, Vancouver and Sydney among others, yet retains a sparkling, lively character of its own.

A DIFFICULT CHOICE

The Hildebrand: elegant, cosy dining.
The Quarterdeck: Malay specialities.
Den Anker: top-class Belgian cuisine.
Belthazar: delicious seafood.
Ocean Basket: variety of seafood.
Quay 4: restaurant and tavern.

ACCOMMODATION

The Table Bay Hotel, tel: 021 406 5000, fax: 406 5977; elegant luxury.
Cape Grace Hotel, tel: 021 410 7100, fax: 419 7622; on the West Quay, with spectacular views.
Victoria and Alfred Hotel, tel: 021 419 6677, fax: 419 8955; Victorian elegance alongside the Alfred Basin; great view of Table Mountain.

Victoria Junction Hotel, Somerset Rd, Green Point, tel: 021 418 1234, fax: 418 5678; avant-garde; loft-style Art Deco.
City Lodge V & A Waterfront, tel: 021 419 9450, fax: 419 0460; convenient, at main entrance to the Waterfront.
One&Only Cape Town, Dock Road, V & A Waterfront, tel: 021 431 5888, fax: 431 5230; urban chic; fine spa.

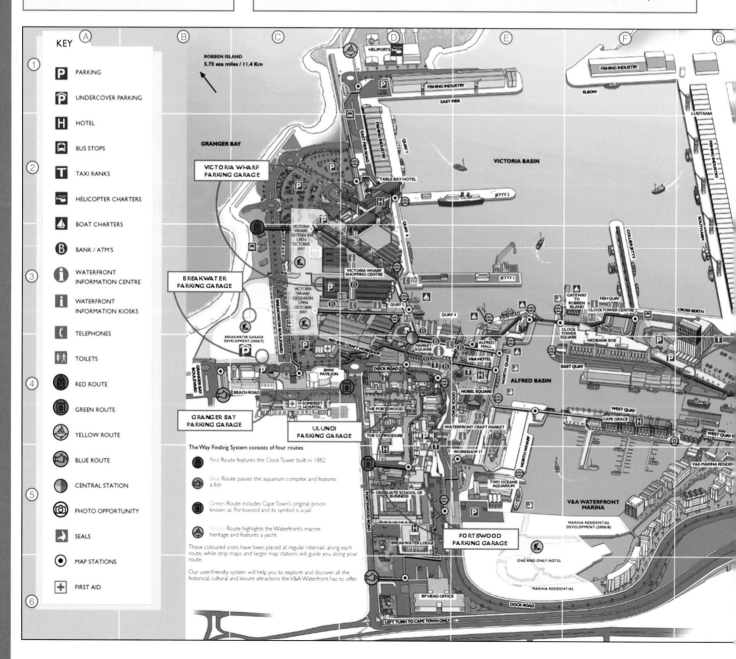

MAIN ATTRACTIONS

Two Oceans Aquarium: an imaginative 35 million-rand complex of world-class standard; watch shoals of fish swim through giant aquariums and explore the touch pools.

Iziko South African Maritime Museum: on 4000m² (13,123ft²); this museum contains the largest display of model ships in South Africa. There is also a discovery cove for the children.

Scratch Patch: an inexpensive fun outing for children; adults also enjoy scratching for gems.

Art and Craft Market: filled with an enormous variety of goods that will appeal to both young and old.

The King's Warehouse: here you can sample the fare of the many diverse food stalls and shop at the huge fish market.

The Red Shed: watch artists at work as they create a variety of items, from delicate glass-blown flowers to colourful ethnic oil paintings and wooden toys.

Cape fur seals: a thriving, wild community of these mammals frequents the calm harbour waters. Watch them diving, lazily floating around, or basking in the sun.

Boat trips: a number of boats and smaller vessels are available for harbour and sunset cruises, as well as longer trips to historic **Robben Island**, the former prison enclave whose most famous inmate was Nelson Mandela.

Concerts: often held at the Amphitheatre; an event calendar is available from information kiosks.

Shops and restaurants: there are plenty of options to choose from, with 400 shops, 70 eateries and also extended opening hours.

Spring Flower Show: landscaping, gardening and flower exhibition, flower carpet, show gardens, floral art displays, a photographic exhibition and a Flower Power Concert; from 3 to 7 September.

Air Charters & Tours, The Hopper: NAC Makana Aviation offer Cape Town's only helicopter experience with single seats. Flights depart from the Waterfront; includes spectacular views of the city, Robben Island, Lion's Head, Table Mountain and surrounds. www.waterfront.co.za

G H I J K

Shopping

Alfred Mall Shopping Centre	E4
Cape Union Mart Adventure Centre	D3
Clock Tower Shopping Centre	F3
King's Warehouse	D3
Musica Megastore	E4
Market Plaza	D4
Nike Concept Store	D4
Pierhead	E3
Red Shed Craft Workshop	D4
Vaughan Johnson's Wine Shop	D4
Victoria Wharf Shopping Centre and Food Court	D3
Waterfront Craft Market and Wellness Centre	E4
Workshop 17	E5

Offices

BP Head Office	D6
Clock Tower Offices	F3
Granger Bay Court	C4
Nedbank BOE Square and Offices	E4
Portswood Square Offices	D4
Village & Life	G5

Historical Sites

Bascule Bridge	E4
Chavonnes Battery	F4
Clock Tower (Built 1882)	E3
Collier Jetty	F3
Dock House	D4
Dragon Tree	D4
Graduate School of Business	D5
Iziko South African Maritime Museum	D4
Old Port Captain's Building	E3
Robinson Dry Dock	E4
Refinery	H5
Synchrolift	G4
Time Ball Tower	D4
Union Castle Building	D4

General

Amphitheatre	D3
Avis Car Rental	F3
Beach Road	C4
Breakwater Boulevard	C4
Clock Tower Square	F3
Coen Steytler Entrance	J5
Croquet Lawns	D4
Dock Road	D6
East Pier Road	D2

East Quay	F4
Ebenezer Entrance	G5
Gateway Tourism Centre	F3
Granger Bay Boulevard Entrance	B4
Granger Bay Boulevard	B4
Marina Residential Show House	E4
Market Square	D4
NSRI	D3
Nobel Square	E4
Passenger Services Terminal	D2
Portswood Road Entrance	D6
Rotunda Entrance (Victoria Wharf)	C2
Schoolbus Parking	C3
Somerset Hospital	C4
South Arm Road	G3
Swing Bridge	E3
Tour Coach Parking (Clock Tower)	G4
Tour Coach Parking (Victoria Wharf)	C3
V&A Marina Residential	G5
Waterfront Information Centre	D4
West Quay	F4
West Quay Road	G4

Leisure Attractions

The Pavilion	C4
Ferrymans and Mitchell's Brewery	D4
Heliports	D1

Jetty 1	D3
Jetty 2	D2
Nelson Mandela Gateway to Robben Island	F3
Quay 4	D3
Quay 5	D3
Quay 6	D2
Robben Island Museum and Ferries	F3
Seal Landing	E3
Scratch Patch	D4
Two Oceans Aquarium	E5

Hotels

Cape Grace	F4
City Lodge V&A Waterfront	I5
Commodore	D4
One&Only Cape Town	E6
Portswood	D4
Protea Hotel Breakwater Lodge	D5
Table Bay	D2
Victoria & Alfred	E4

Fishing

Fish Quay	F3
North Quay	E4
North Wharf	E4

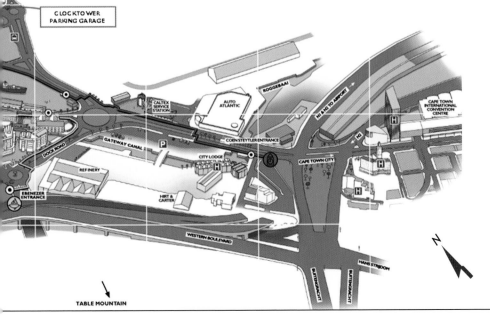

www.waterfront.co.za

Free State

This rather dry, mostly flat and largely treeless east-central region of South Africa offers the visitor a number of appealing destinations, from game reserves teeming with a variety of wildlife to the evocative Bushman rock paintings along the eastern escarpment. Mine dumps greet your arrival at towns like Welkom, Allanridge and Virginia, all of which have grown up around the gold-fields that were opened up shortly after World War II.

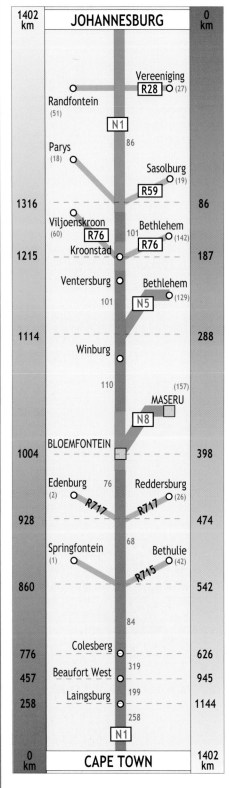

Main Attractions

Bloemfontein: attractive and vibrant capital of the Free State.
Maria Moroka Nature Reserve: a pleasant mountain reserve, near the small town of **Thaba 'Nchu** and sanctuary for antelope and other wildlife; splendid scenery.
Golden Gate Highlands National Park: scenic wildlife reserve with dramatically sculpted sandstone ridges and cliffs.
The Vaal Dam: 300km^2 (116-sq-mile) stretch of water, popular with boating enthusiasts and fishermen.
Willem Pretorius Nature Reserve: game reserve between Winburg and Ventersburg; variety of wildlife including white rhino, giraffe and buffalo; tel: 057 651 4168.
Gariep Dam: the country's largest water reservoir; near Bethulie.
Gariep Dam Nature Reserve: located on the vast dam's northern shore; home to a very large population of graceful springbok.

Accommodation

Protea Hotel Black Mountain, Groothoek Dam Rd, Thaba 'Nchu District, tel: 051 871 4200, fax: 873 2521.
Welkom Inn, Welkom, tel: 057 357 3361, fax: 352 1458.
De Stijl Gariep Hotel, Gariep Dam, tel: 051 754 0060, fax: 754 0268.
Hacienda Hotel, Kroonstad, tel: 056 212 5111, fax: 213 3298.

Below: *This visually bare landscape, near Kroonstad, is typical of the Free State. Here, a rain-laden sky dominates the great, undulating grasslands, punctuated by a solitary windmill.*

Travel Tips

The Free State's main roads are in good condition, linking this central region with other major South African cities. Please note: distances between towns are vast, so be sure to fill up with petrol regularly.

Useful Contacts

Universitas Hospital, Bloemfontein, tel: 051 506 3500, fax: 444 5499.
Free State Tourism, Bloemfontein, tel: 051 411 4300, fax: 444 0297.
Kimberley Information Centre, tel: 053 832 7298, fax: 832 7211.

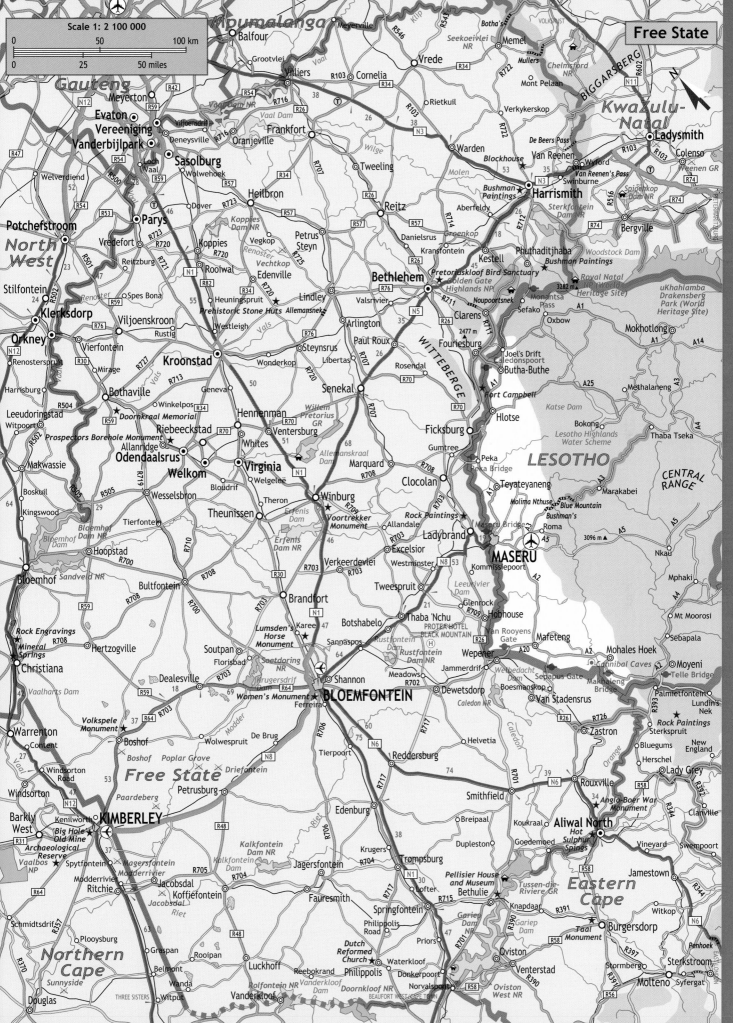

Scale 1: 2 100 000

Bloemfontein

Bloemfontein is the judicial capital of South Africa and the principal city of the Free State. The most centrally situated of South Africa's major cities, it lies at the heart of an area of fertile farmland 1392m (4567ft) above sea level and owes much of its prosperity to the Free State goldfields, located 160km (100 miles) to the northeast. The city is noted for its impressive old buildings, museums, monuments, memorials and public parks and gardens.

ACCOMMODATION

Southern Sun Bloemfontein, tel: 051 444 1253.
Protea Hotel Bloemfontein Central, East Burger Street, tel: 051 403 8000, fax: 447 7102.
Protea Hotel Bloemfontein, 202 Nelson Mandela Drive, tel: 051 444 4321.
President Hotel, tel: 051 430 1111, fax: 430 4141; at the foot of Naval Hill.

MAIN ATTRACTIONS

Franklin Nature Reserve: on Naval Hill; home to a variety of wildlife.
National Botanical Garden: pleasant floral sanctuary dominated by impressive dolomite outcrops.
Orchid House: pools, waterfalls and over 3000 exquisite orchids at the foot of Naval Hill.
Loch Logan Waterfront: shops, restaurants and events.
National Women's Memorial: in memory of the more than 27,000 Boer women and children who died in British concentration camps during the Anglo-Boer War.

First Raadsaal: the old town hall, housed in a lovely building.
Sand du Plessis Theatre: modern complex; the splendid works of art contribute to the decor.
Soetdoring Nature Reserve: on the R64 to Kimberley; protective habitat for antelope, lion, cheetah and brown hyena.
National Afrikaans Literary Museum: in the Old Government Building; a treasure house of African literature, with manuscripts, etc., belonging to well-known South African writers. Also houses the Afrikaans Music Museum (musical instruments) and Theatre Museum.

TRAVEL TIPS

Bloemfontein is on the main north-south highway, the N1, which links Cape Town to Johannesburg. Good tarred roads connect the city with all the surrounding major centres, such as Welkom (R700 and R710); Kimberley (R64); Maseru in Lesotho (R64); and East London on the coast (R30).

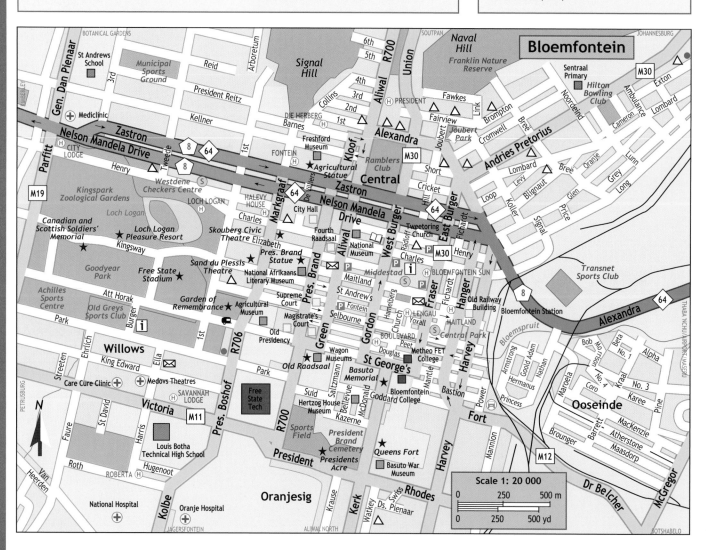

Kimberley

Kimberley, the world-renowned diamond centre and capital of neighbouring Northern Cape province, was born in the 1870s when tens of thousands of prospectors poured into the area to unearth the glittering gems that lay in abundance beneath the dusty ground. Kimberley still retains much of the old-world atmosphere of these heady days, when instant fortunes were made (and lost), and money and champagne flowed like water.

ACCOMMODATION

Garden Court Kimberley, tel: 053 833 1751, fax: 832 1814; in a lovely garden setting.
Hotel Kimberlite, tel: 053 831 1968; within easy walking distance of the Big Hole.
Horseshoe Motel, Memorial Road, tel: 053 832 5267.

Right: When diamond fever struck in 1871, no one could have guessed that 43 years later the Big Hole would reach a depth of 1097m (3600ft). Between 1871 and 1914, 22.6 million tons of earth was excavated from the mine for a yield of 2722kg (6000lb) of diamonds.

MAIN ATTRACTIONS

The Big Hole: Kimberley's historic hub. By the time it was closed in 1914 it had yielded almost three tons of diamonds.
Kimberley Mine Museum: evocative and comprehensive insight into the town's lively past.
Duggan-Cronin Gallery: an outstanding photographic display of the San-Bushman culture.
William Humphreys Gallery: an excellent collection of South African and European paintings, sculpture and furniture.
The Diggers Fountain: honours the miners who helped to build the Diamond City.
Magersfontein battlefield: for directions, call tel: 053 833 7115.
Star of the West: this public house was the favorite rendezvous of diamond prospectors from the early 1870s. Has a stool said to have been made specially for Cecil Rhodes.

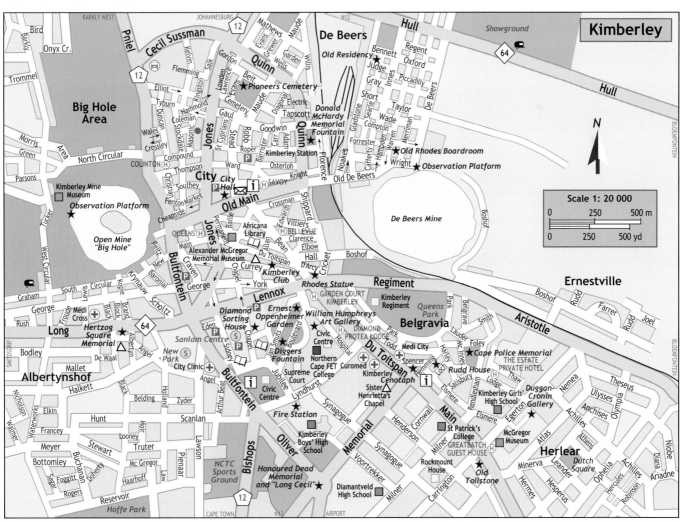

Main Map Section Key and Legend

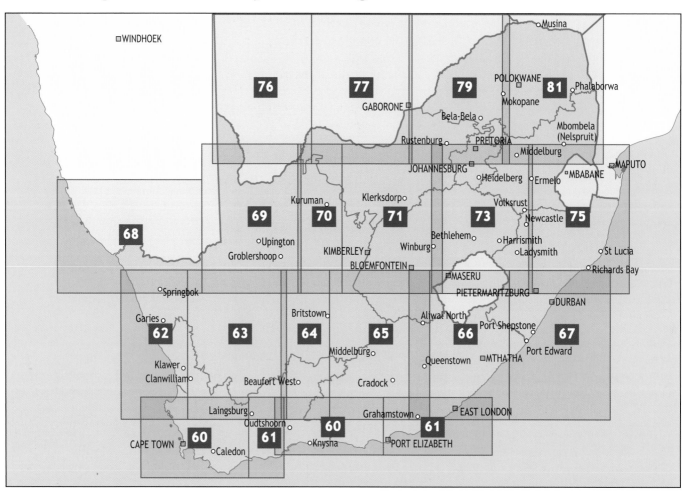

Pages 60-61		0	50	100 km
Scale 1: 1 790 000				
		0	25	50 miles

Pages 62-81		0	50	100 km
Scale 1: 1 600 000				
		0	25	50 miles

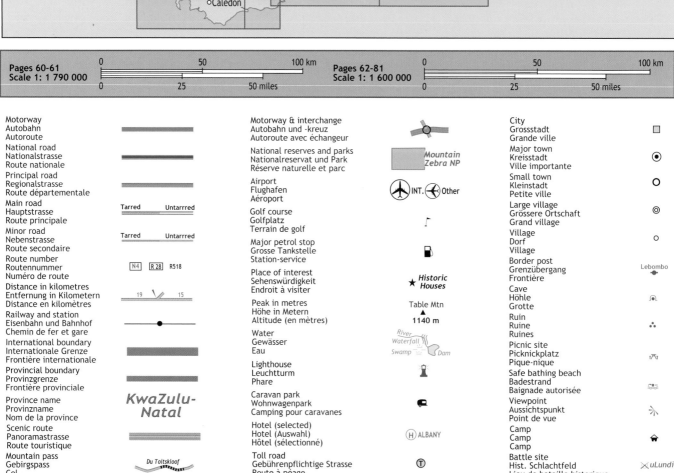

Motorway / Autobahn / Autoroute

Motorway & interchange / Autobahn und -kreuz / Autoroute avec échangeur

City / Grossstadt / Grande ville

National road / Nationalstrasse / Route nationale

National reserves and parks / Nationalreservat und Park / Réserve naturelle et parc — *Mountain Zebra NP*

Major town / Kreisstadt / Ville importante

Principal road / Regionalstrasse / Route départementale

Airport / Flughafen / Aéroport — INT. / Other

Small town / Kleinstadt / Petite ville

Main road / Hauptstrasse / Route principale — Tarred Untarrred

Golf course / Golfplatz / Terrain de golf

Large village / Grössere Ortschaft / Grand village

Minor road / Nebenstrasse / Route secondaire — Tarred Untarrred

Major petrol stop / Grosse Tankstelle / Station-service

Village / Dorf / Village

Route number / Routennummer / Numéro de route — N4 R 28 R518

Place of interest / Sehenswürdigkeit / Endroit à visiter

Border post / Grenzübergang / Frontière — Lebombo

Distance in kilometres / Entfernung in Kilometern / Distance en kilomètres — 19 — 15

Peak in metres / Höhe in Metern / Altitude (en mètres) — *Historic Houses* Table Mtn ▲ 1140 m

Cave / Höhle / Grotte

Railway and station / Eisenbahn und Bahnhof / Chemin de fer et gare

Water / Gewässer / Eau — *River Waterfall Swamp Dam*

Ruin / Ruine / Ruines

International boundary / Internationale Grenze / Frontière internationale

Lighthouse / Leuchtturm / Phare

Picnic site / Picknickplatz / Pique-nique

Provincial boundary / Provinzgrenze / Frontière provinciale

Caravan park / Wohnwagenpark / Camping pour caravanes

Safe bathing beach / Badestrand / Baignade autorisée

Province name / Provinzname / Nom de la province — *KwaZulu-Natal*

Hotel (selected) / Hotel (Auswahl) / Hôtel (sélectionné) — ℍ ALBANY

Viewpoint / Aussichtspunkt / Point de vue

Scenic route / Panoramastrasse / Route touristique

Toll road / Gebührenpflichtige Strasse / Route à péage — T

Camp / Camp / Camp

Mountain pass / Gebirgspass / Col — *Du Toitskloof*

Battle site / Hist. Schlachtfeld / Lieu de bataille historique — uLundi

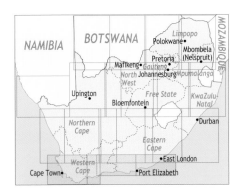

Eastern and Western Cape

Dominated by series after series of soaring mountain ranges interspersed with rolling wheat fields, orchards and vineyards, the southern part of South Africa is one of the continent's most beautiful regions. Inland there are forests, deep fertile valleys and spectacular mountain passes to explore, while the rugged, rocky coastline offers the visitor countless venues for safe bathing, surfing, beachcombing and fishing, together with a number of delightful holiday villages and towns. So gloriously abundant is the flora of this particular stretch of South African coastline that it has been named the Garden Route.

MAIN ATTRACTIONS

Wineland towns: wide, tree-lined avenues and historic buildings.
Day drives: along the southern coastline; two are particularly recommended: from Cape Town to the little town of Hermanus, haven for southern right whales; and from Cape Town to Langebaan Lagoon on the West Coast, renowned for its bird life.
The Garden Route: from Mossel Bay to the Storms River, scenically one of the

most splendid parts of the South African coastline; visit the towns of Knysna and Plettenberg Bay.
Hex River Valley: dramatic sandstone crags dominate the green, beautiful valley, where excellent grapes are cultivated.
The Klein Karoo: a beautiful and rugged region lying between the southern coastal rampart and the Swartberg uplands to the north.

TRAVEL TIPS

The N2 national route leads eastward along the south coast from Cape Town to East London, and is the best way to see

the beautiful South African countryside. The road is wide and in excellent condition and petrol stations are frequent.

Below: *A myriad vineyards have been established in the fertile soils of the beautiful Hex River Valley.*

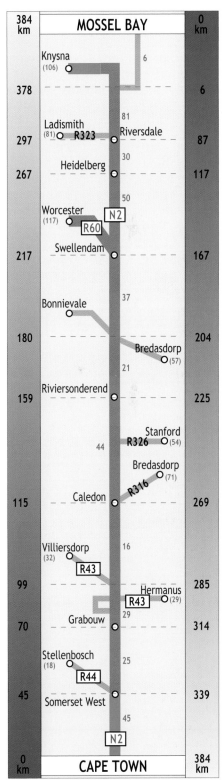

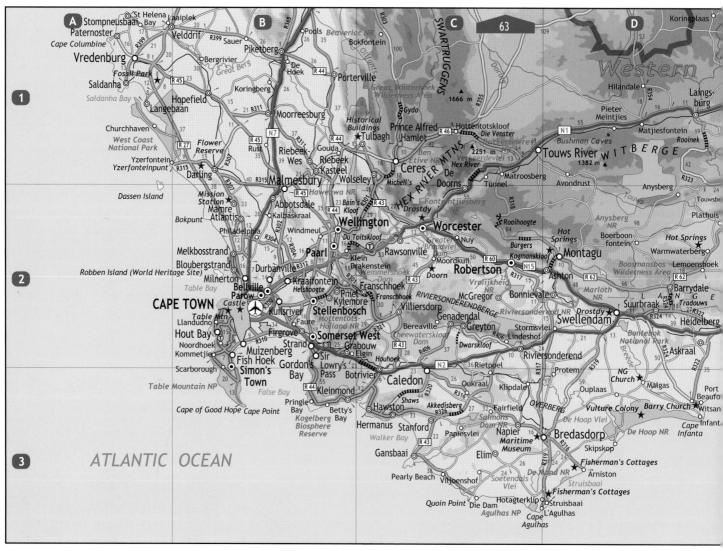

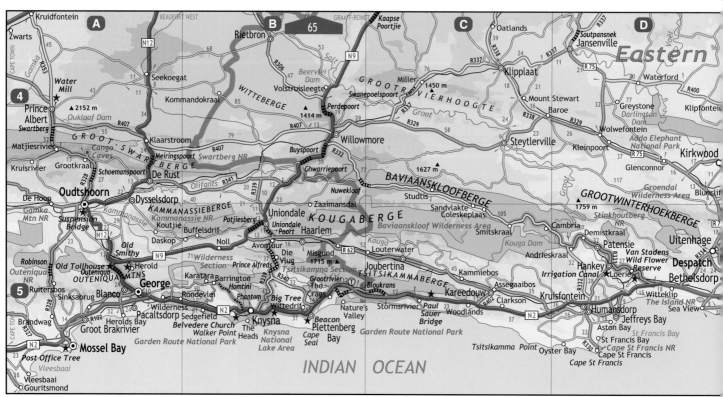

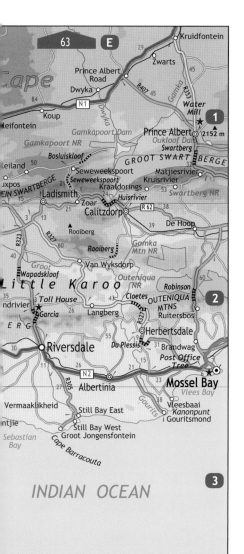

Above: *The scenic splendour of Knysna Lagoon has ensured the resort town's popularity, and the lagoon is lined with many attractive homes and holiday retreats in garden settings.*

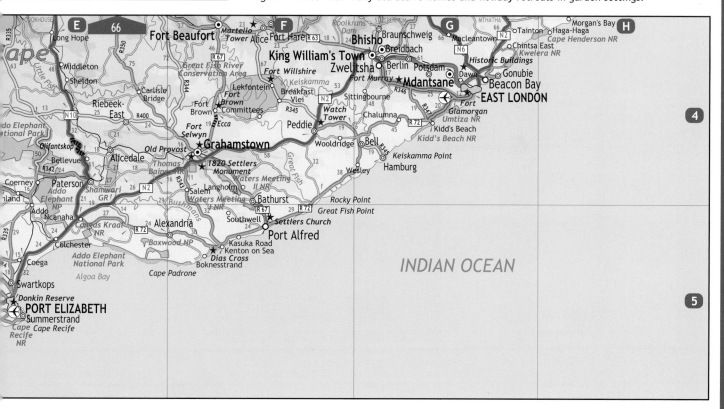

NAMIBIA • BOTSWANA
Limpopo
Polokwane •
Mafikeng • • Mbombela (Nelspruit)
North • Pretoria
West • Johannesburg • Mpumalanga
Gauteng
Upington • Free State • KwaZulu-Natal
Bloemfontein • Durban
Northern Cape • East London
Eastern Cape
Western Cape
Cape Town • • Port Elizabeth

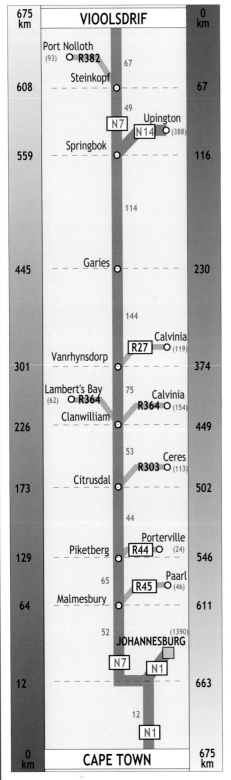

675 km	VIOOLSDRIF	0 km
	Port Nolloth (93) ○ R382	
	67	
608	Steinkopf	67
	49	
	N7	Upington
	N14	(388)
559	Springbok	116
	114	
445	Garies	230
	144	
	R27	Calvinia (119)
301	Vanrhynsdorp	374
	75	
	Lambert's Bay (62) ○ R364	Calvinia R364 ○ (154)
226	Clanwilliam	449
	53	
	R303	Ceres ○ (113)
173	Citrusdal	502
	44	
	R44	Porterville ○ (24)
129	Piketberg	546
	65	
	R45	Paarl ○ (46)
64	Malmesbury	611
	52	(1390)
	JOHANNESBURG	
	N7	N1
12		663
	12	
	N1	
0 km	CAPE TOWN	675 km

Port Nolloth ★
Mc Dougall's Bay
Wedge Point
Discovery of First Diamond in Namaqualand

A — 93 — R382 — Windpoort — VIOOLSDRIF — B — 68 — C — N14

Bulletrap — 44
Nigramoep — Orbicular Diorite Koppie ★ Concordia
Grootmis — 93 R355 — Nababeep — Okiep — Goegap Nature Reserve — 109
Langbaai — Miners' Memorial ★ — ★ Van der Stel's Copper Mine 1685
Kleinsee — Springbok
Melkbospunt — Komaggas — Spektakel — Mesklip — 72 R355 — Uitkyk
Burke's
Messelpad — Gamoep
Namaqua National Park — Wildeperdehoek
Skulpfonteinpunt — Soebatsfontein — 114 — Scenic Route: Wild flowers in Spring (Aug-Sep) — Pypmaker se Poort
Skilpad Wildflower Gardens ★ — Kamieskroon — 43
Koingnaas — ★ Barter's Grave — Kamiesberg — Stofvlei
Dokter se Baai — Spoegrivier — Witwater — Platbakkies
Hondeklipbaai — Karkams — 37
Wallekraal — Alwynsfontein
Rooiwal Bay — Northern Cape — Garies — Kliprand
Strandfonteinpunt — Grootberg 1022 m
Galjoen Bay — Groen — 74 — 85 — Rooiwalspoort
Nariep — Western Cape
Groenriviersmond — R358 — 875 m
Island Point — Rietpoort
Kotzesrus — Bitterfontein

ATLANTIC OCEAN

Komkans — Nuwerus
Blinkwater Bay — 60 — R363 — 70 — N7
Landplaas — Scenic Route: Wild flowers in Spring (Aug-Sep)
Lutzville — Vanrhynsdorp
Olifants — R362 — 27 — R27
Papendorp — 24 — Vredendal — 31
Strandfontein — R27 — Klawer
Doringbaai — Olifants River Irrigation Scheme — Trawal
Heerenlogement Cave — 55
Rooiduinepunt — Heerenlogement
Ratelfontein
Lambert's Bay — R364 — Graafwater
Leipoldtville — R365
Elandsbaai NR — Sandberg
Elandsbaai
Baboon Point — R27
Redelinghuys
Noordkuil
Rocherpan NR — Dwarskersbos — Aurora
St Helena Bay — PIKETBERG
Stompneus Bay — 67 — R399
Stompneuspunt — St Helena Bay — Velddrif — Sauer
Paternoster — Vredenburg — R399 — Bergrivier
60 — R79 — Fossil Park ★ — R27 — Grootrivier
Saldanha — R45 — Hopefield

Above: *The reliable donkey cart is still the preferred mode of transport for most farm workers wishing to travel through the arid expanse of Namaqualand.*

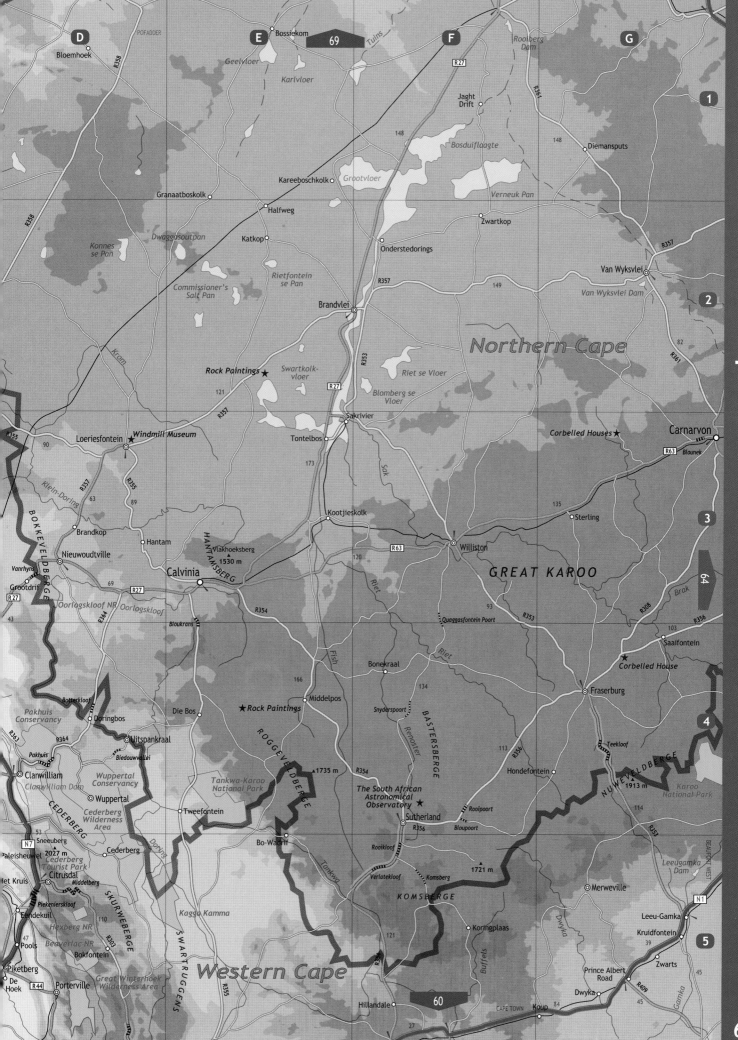

D

Bloemhoek

POFADDER

Bossiekom E

Tuins

69

F

Jaght
Drift

R27

Rooiberg
Dam

G

1

R358

Geelvloer

Karlvloer

148

Bosduiflaagte

148

Diemansputs

Konnes
se Pan

Dwaggasoutpan

Granaatboskolk

Halfweg

Katkop

Grootvloer

Kareeboschkolk

Onderstedorings

Verneuk Pan

Zwartkop

R357

R361

Van Wyksvlei

R358

Commissioner's
Salt Pan

Rietfontein
se Pan

Krom

Brandvlei

R357

Swartkolk-
vloer

121

R357

R27

Sakrivier

Tontelbos

R353

Riet se Vloer

Blomberg se
Vloer

Northern Cape

149

82

R361

2

Van Wyksvlei Dam

Rock Paintings ★

R355

90

Loeriesfontein

Windmill Museum ★

173

Klein-Doring

R357

63

R355

89

Brandkop

Hantam

Kootjieskolk

Sak

Corbelled Houses ★

R63

Carnarvon

Blaunek

135

Sterling

Bokkeveldberge

Nieuwoudtville

Vanrhyns

Grootdrif
R27

43

R355

R357

HANTAMSBERG

Vlakhoeksberg
▲ 1530 m

Calvinia

R63

120

Williston

GREAT KAROO

Brak

64

3

R308

R356

103

Saaifontein

Oorlogskloof NR Oorlogskloof

69

R27

R364

Bloukrans

R354

Fish

Riet

93

R353

Quaggasfontein Poort

Riet

Corbelled House ★

Fraserburg

4

Botterkloof

Pakhuis
Conservancy

Doringbos

R363

R364

Uitspankraal

Pakhuis

Biedouwvallei

Clanwilliam

Clanwliam Dam

Wuppertal
Conservancy

Wuppertal

166

Die Bos

★ Rock Paintings

Middelpos

ROGGEVELDBERGE

134

Snyderspoort

Bonekraal

BASTERSBERGE

Renoster

113

R356

Hondefontein

Teekloof

NUWEVELDBERGE

▲ 1913 m

Karoo
National Park

CEDERBERG

Cederberg
Wilderness
Area

53

Sneeuberg
▲ 2027 m
Cederberg
Tourist Park

Citrusdal

Middelberg

Cederberg

Doring

Tweefontein

▲ 1735 m

R354

Tankwa-Karoo
National Park

The South African
Astronomical
Observatory ★

Sutherland

R356

Rooipoort

Bloupoort

114

R353

Leeugamka
Dam

BEAUFORT WEST

Paleisheuwel

N7

et Kruis

Piekenierskloof

Eendekuil

Hexberg NR

47

Pools

Beaverlac NR

Piketberg

De
Hoek

R44

Porterville

SKURWEBERGE

110

R303

Bokfontein

Great Winterhoek
Wilderness Area

SWARTRUGGENS

Kagga Kamma

Bo-Wadrif

Tankwa

Rooikloof

Verlatekloof

Komsberg

Komsberg

▲ 1721 m

KOMSBERGE

Koringplaas

121

Buffels

Dwyka

Merweville

N1

Leeu-Gamka

Kruidfontein

39

R409

Zwarts

45

5

Western Cape

60

Hillandale

27

CAPE TOWN

Koup

84

Koup

Dwyka

Prince Albert
Road

R355

R355

Gamka

45

Great Karoo

This semi-arid region of bone-dry air, minimal rainfall and intense sunshine dominates the Cape interior. The countryside stretches endlessly to the distant horizons, dotted with lonely windmills and isolated farmsteads.

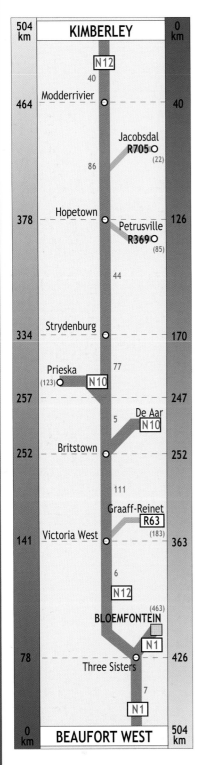

MAIN ATTRACTIONS

Beaufort West: birthplace of the famed heart surgeon Chris Barnard; this little town is also noted for its lovely pear-tree-lined streets.

Karoo National Park: north of Beaufort West; wildlife includes mountain zebra, shy leopard and antelope.

Graaff-Reinet: third oldest town in the Cape, with some fine old architecture.

Valley of Desolation: near Graaff-Reinet; a fantasia of wind-eroded, strangely shaped dolerite peaks, pillars and balancing rocks.

Nieu-Bethesda: tiny hamlet, 50km (31 miles) north of Graaff-Reinet; home to the Owl House Museum's bizarre sculptures, many of which are decorated with ground glass.

Cradock: in the vicinity are the Mountain Zebra National Park and author Olive Schreiner's grave.

Aliwal North: this pleasant town to the far east of the Great Karoo has hot sulphur springs and an excellent spa.

A   B   75   C   D

1

Redcliffe · Rosetta · ESTCOURT
Kamberg ☐ Nottingham Road · New Hanover · 72 · R33
uKhahlamba · Karkloof NR · Dalton
Drakensberg Park · Albert Falls NR · EMPANGENI · Tugela Mouth
(World Heritage Site) · Lidgetton · **Howick** · Midmar Dam NR · Mpolweni · R614 · 114 · Darnall · Ultimatum Tree · Fort Pearson
iMpendle · Hilton · Midmar NR · 64 · N3 · **KwaDukuza** · Shaka's Memorial ★★
Nzuze · Groutville · Blythdale Beach
Edendale · **PIETERMARITZBURG** · Ndwedwe · Shakaskraal · 33 · Salt Rock
Thornville · Natal Lion Park · Tongaat · Shaka's Rock
R617 · Kranskloof NR · iNanda · 42 · Ballito
Bulwer · **Mpumalanga** · 81 · **Verulam** · uMhlanga
R612 · Richmond · Hammarsdale · **KwaMashu**
75 · Donnybrook · R624 · R603 · **Pinetown** · **DURBAN**
Creighton · ★ Bush Reserve · 80 · R624 · **Queensburgh** · The Bluff
Riverside · R56 · Rosebank · **uMlazi**
CJ Rhodes' House ★ · **iSipingo**
iXopo · Mkomazi · **Kingsburgh** · uMbogintwini
Mzimvubu · 62 · **aManzimtoti**
Highflats · Vernon Crookes NR · uMgababa
Umzimkulu · R612 · 88 · **uMzinto** · uMkomaas
KwaZulu-Natal · Braemar · Scottburgh
61 · Bisi · Park Rynie
Stafford's Post · St Faith's · Sezela
Bontrand · KwaDweshula · 59 · Mtwalume
Weza · Harding · N2 · Hibberdene
Oribi Gorge NR · R100
129 · Bizana · Marburg · Sea Park
Redoubt · Paddock · uMtentweni
R61 · **Port Shepstone**
Munster · uVongo
Impisi · Banner Rest · Margate
Umtamvuna NR · Ramsgate
Southbroom
Glenmore Beach
Port Edward
Umtentu
Mkambati Nature Reserve
Mkambati
South Sand Bluff
Port Grosvenor
Mbotyi

INDIAN OCEAN

2

3

Above: *The wide mouth of the Mgeni River, in Durban, is spanned by several bridges. The renowned Mgeni River Bird Park, which houses some 300 exotic and local species and is rated the third best in the world, is accessible via the Mgeni River Bridge from OR Tambo Parade.*

NAMIBIA · BOTSWANA · Limpopo · MOZAMBIQUE
Polokwane ·
Mbombela (Nelspruit) ·
Mafikeng · Pretoria · Gauteng
North West · Johannesburg · Mpumalanga
Upington · Free State · KwaZulu-Natal
Bloemfontein · Durban
Northern Cape · Eastern Cape
Western Cape · East London
Cape Town · Port Elizabeth

4

5

Northern Cape

*M*uch of this region — the western part — is a dry, rather forbidding moonscape of low mountains and strange plants like the kokerboom. After the rainy season, however, the arid veld is transformed into a riot of colour as wild flowers bloom in abundance. Towns are few and small, with the exception of Upington, which is beautifully situated along the banks of the Orange River.

TRAVEL TIPS

The main highways that service the northern and northwestern Cape, and those which traverse the vast Karoo region, are generally in good condition. Note: be sure to stop for petrol and refreshments in good time, as the towns (and the service stations) tend to lie rather far apart in this region. Beware of wild animals crossing the road, especially at dawn, dusk and at night.

MAIN ATTRACTIONS

Upington: visit one of the dried fruit co-ops around the town.
Augrabies Falls National Park: marvel at the lovely waterfall (one of the five biggest in the world) in this otherwise harsh area, and drive through the reserve to spot the bird- and wildlife.
Kgalagadi Transfrontier National Park: straddles the South Africa–Botswana border north of Upington. This is the first of Africa's 'peace parks'. The red sand dunes of the southern segment, shy Kalahari lion, an abundance of raptor species, and magnificent sunsets attract nature lovers to this unique desert park.
Goegap Nature Reserve: east of Springbok; spot eland, springbok and mountain zebra along hiking trails and game drives.
Richtersveld National Park: in the far northwestern corner of the province; hauntingly beautiful.
Vioolsdrif/Noordoewer: South Africa–Namibia border post, for travellers heading to Namibia.

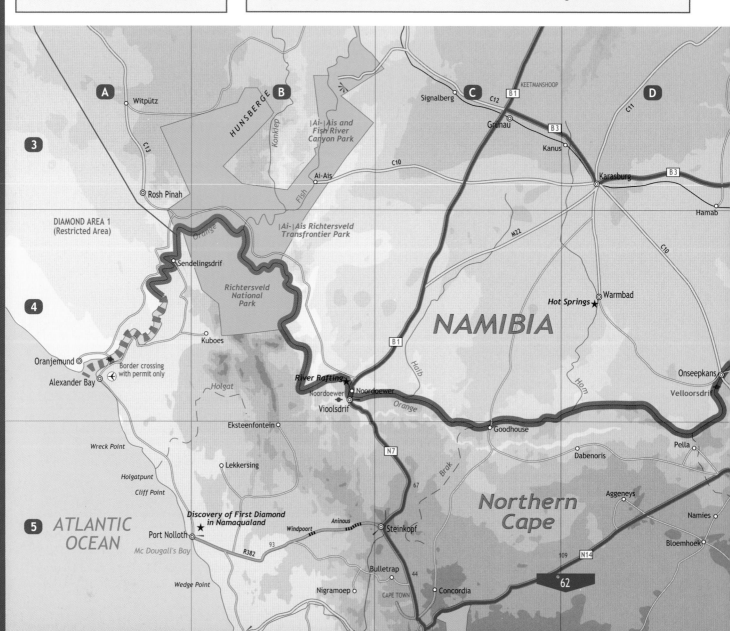

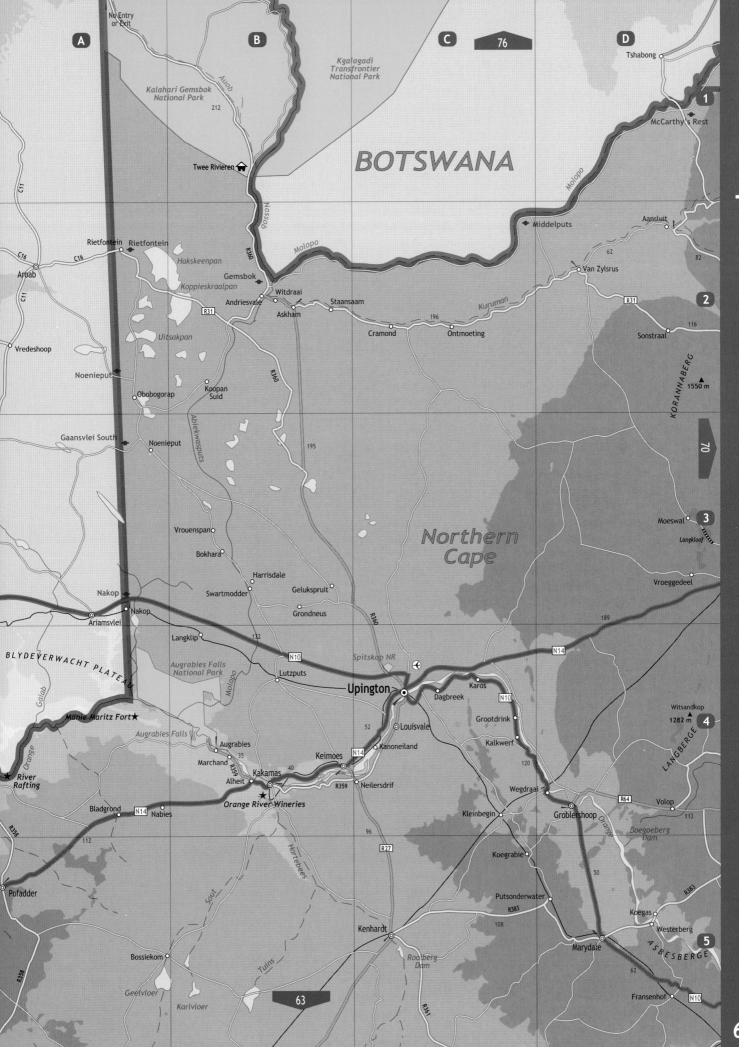

A
B
C
76
D

No Entry or Exit

1

Tshabong

McCarthy's Rest

Kgalagadi Transfrontier National Park

BOTSWANA

Kalahari Gemsbok National Park

212

Auob

Twee Rivieren

Nossob

Molopo

Middelputs

Aansluit

62

82

C11

C16

Rietfontein Rietfontein

C16

Aroab

C11

Hakskeenpan

Gemsbok

Witdraai

R360

Molopo

Van Zylsrus

R31

2

Koppieskraalpan

Andriesvale

R31

Staansaam

Kuruman

Sonstraal

116

Vredeshoop

Askham

Cramond

Ontmoeting

196

Uitsakpan

Noenieput

KORANNABERG

Koopan Suid

R360

1550 m

Obobogorap

195

70

Gaansvlei South

Noenieput

Abiekwasputs

Moeswal

3

Langkloof

Vrouenspan

Northern Cape

Vroeggedeel

Bokhara

Harrisdale

Swartmodder

Gelukspruit

R360

189

Nakop

Grondneus

BLYDEVERWACHT PLATEAU

Langklip

132

Nakop

N10

Spitskop NR

N14

Ariamsvlei

Gaiab

Augrabies Falls National Park

Lutzputs

Upington

Karos

N10

Witsandkop

Manie Maritz Fort★

Molopo

Dagbreek

1282 m

4

Augrabies Falls

Louisvale

Grootdrink

LANGBERGE

Orange

52

Augrabies

35

Kanoneiland

Kalkwerf

River Rafting

Marchand

R359

Keimoes

N14

Neilersdrif

120

Wegdraai

R64

Volop

Kakamas

40

R359

Alheit

Orange River Wineries

113

Bladgrond

N14

Nabies

96

Kleinbegin

Groblershoop

Orange

Boegoeberg Dam

R358

112

R27

Koegrabie

R383

50

Pofadder

Hartebees

Putsonderwater

Koegas

Westerberg

R383

Sout

108

ASBESBERGE

Bossiekom

Kenhardt

Marydale

5

Tuins

Rooiberg Dam

62

N10

Geelvloer

Karlvloer

63

R361

Fransenhof

N10

Kimberley and Bloemfontein

*T*hese neighbouring
towns, the capitals
of the Northern Cape and
Free State provinces
respectively, are situated
on the high interior
plateau. Both offer fine
museums and sandstone
buildings of historical
interest and are sur-
rounded by nature
reserves and dams.

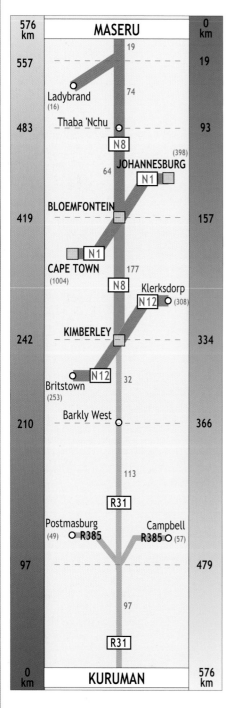

576 km		MASERU		0 km
557		19		19
		Ladybrand (16)	74	
483		Thaba 'Nchu		93
		N8		
		JOHANNESBURG	(398)	
	64	N1		
		BLOEMFONTEIN		
419				157
		N1		
		CAPE TOWN (1004)	177	
		N8		
		N12	Klerksdorp (308)	
		KIMBERLEY		
242				334
		N12	32	
		Britstown (253)		
210		Barkly West		366
		113		
		R31		
		Postmasburg (49) R385	Campbell R385 (57)	
97				479
		97		
		R31		
0 km		KURUMAN		576 km

RUDOLPH DE WET
54 - 1922

Above: The statue of
Christiaan Rudolph de
Wet stands in front of
Bloemfontein's Fourth
Raadsaal, the last government
seat of the old Republic.
Below: The Kimberley Mine
Museum portrays life on the
diamond fields more than a
century ago.

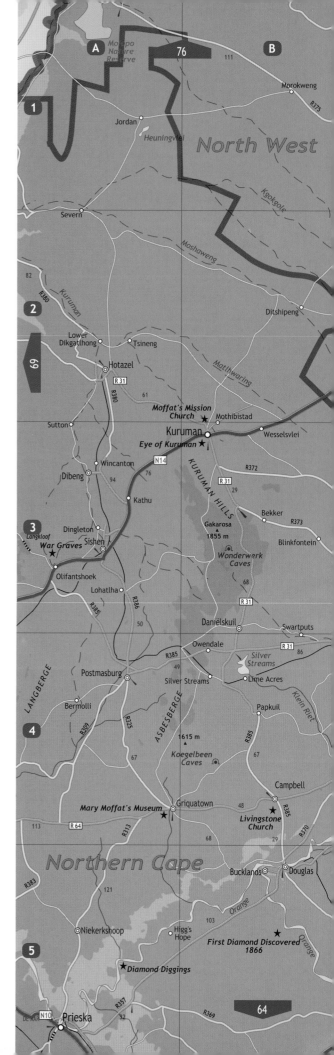

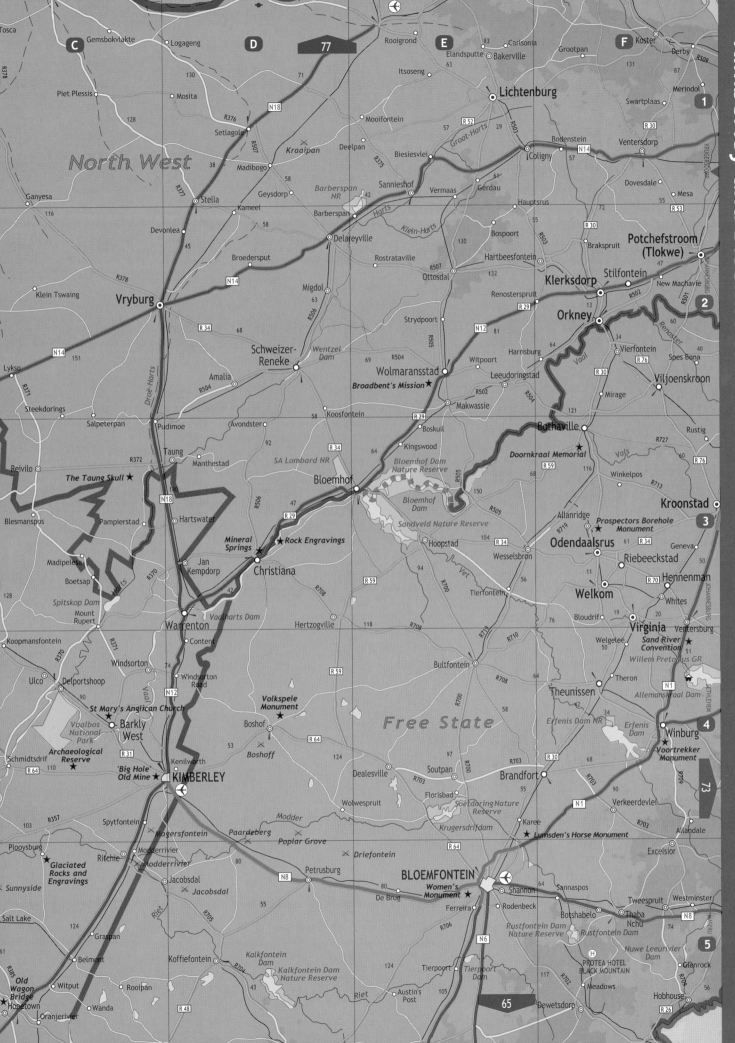

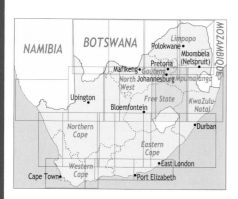

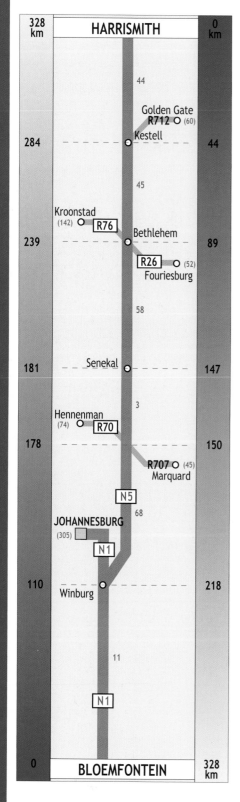

Northeastern Free State

Though much of the Free State consists of flat, treeless grassland plain, the eastern and southern parts are scenically enchanting, rising in a series of picturesquely weathered sandstone hills, and culminating in the high Maluti Mountains of Lesotho in the east. The countryside is at its most spectacular, perhaps, in the Golden Gate Highlands National Park. This is a fertile region, kind to the growers of maize and wheat, sunflowers, fruit (notably cherries) and vegetables. To the north, around Welkom, there are rich deposits of gold.

MAIN ATTRACTIONS

Golden Gate Highlands National Park: south of Bethlehem; sandstone ridges sculpted by the elements; see antelope and over 160 bird species.
Vaal River: border between the Free State and Gauteng; good boating and fishing, especially on the Vaal Dam.

Willem Pretorius Game Reserve: good game-viewing (white rhino and buffalo) near Ventersburg; tel: 057 651 4003.
Pretoriuskloof Bird Sanctuary: near Bethlehem; tel: 058 303 2211.
Bushman paintings: in the Phutha-ditjhaba area, close to Lesotho.

Below: *Travellers are often greeted by large fields of glorious golden yellow sunflowers along the Free State roads. These constitute a major crop in the region which has rich soil, despite relatively poor rainfall and very little surface water.*

Northern KwaZulu-Natal

*T*he midlands and northern parts of KwaZulu-Natal, overlooked by the Drakensberg massif to the west, are noted for their rolling green hills, rich farmlands, charming country towns — and for their place in the military annals. For much of the 1800s this region served as an immense battleground as three nations fought bitterly for mastery of the land. Closer to the coast lie the splendours of the iSimangaliso Wetland Park (St Lucia) and some of Africa's very finest wildlife reserves. The seaboard is popular among fisherman and boating enthusiasts; offshore lie the world's southernmost coral reefs, a magnet for scuba divers.

324 km	EMPANGENI	0 km
	46	
	R34	
	Gingindlovu (51)	
	R66	
278	Nkwalini	46
	R66	
	27	
	uLundi (53)	
	R66	
251	Melmoth	73
	93	
	R68	
158	Silutshana	166
	72	
	Vryheid (67)	
	R33	
86		238
	2	
84	Dundee	240
	26	
	R68	
	Newcastle (42)	
58		266
	58	
	N11	
0 km	LADYSMITH	324 km

Above: *The Ithala Game Reserve, a 30,000ha (74,000-acre) wildlife sanctuary located along the lush banks of the Pongola River, is a haven for the white, or square-lipped, rhino, a highly endangered species. The term 'white' derives from the Afrikaans word 'wyd' (wide) describing the broad, squarish mouth of this mammal.*

MAIN ATTRACTIONS

Howick Falls: outside of Howick, the Mgeni River plunges some 100m (328ft) into a rock pool.

Hluhluwe and iMfolozi Game Reserves: the oldest of South Africa's wildlife sanctuaries, these parks sustain a great number of animals and some 400 species of bird. Tel: 035 562 0848 or 550 8476.

Ithala Game Reserve: home to some 70 species of mammal, among them both white and black rhino, zebra, giraffe, elephant, brown hyena and various antelope. Beautiful Ntshondwe rest camp is just one accommodation alternative that is available here. Tel: 034 983 2540.

Phinda Resource Reserve: an up-market ecotourist venture that shares its resources with the local communities, while providing the visitor with an exhilarating wilderness experience. Tel: 035 562 0271.

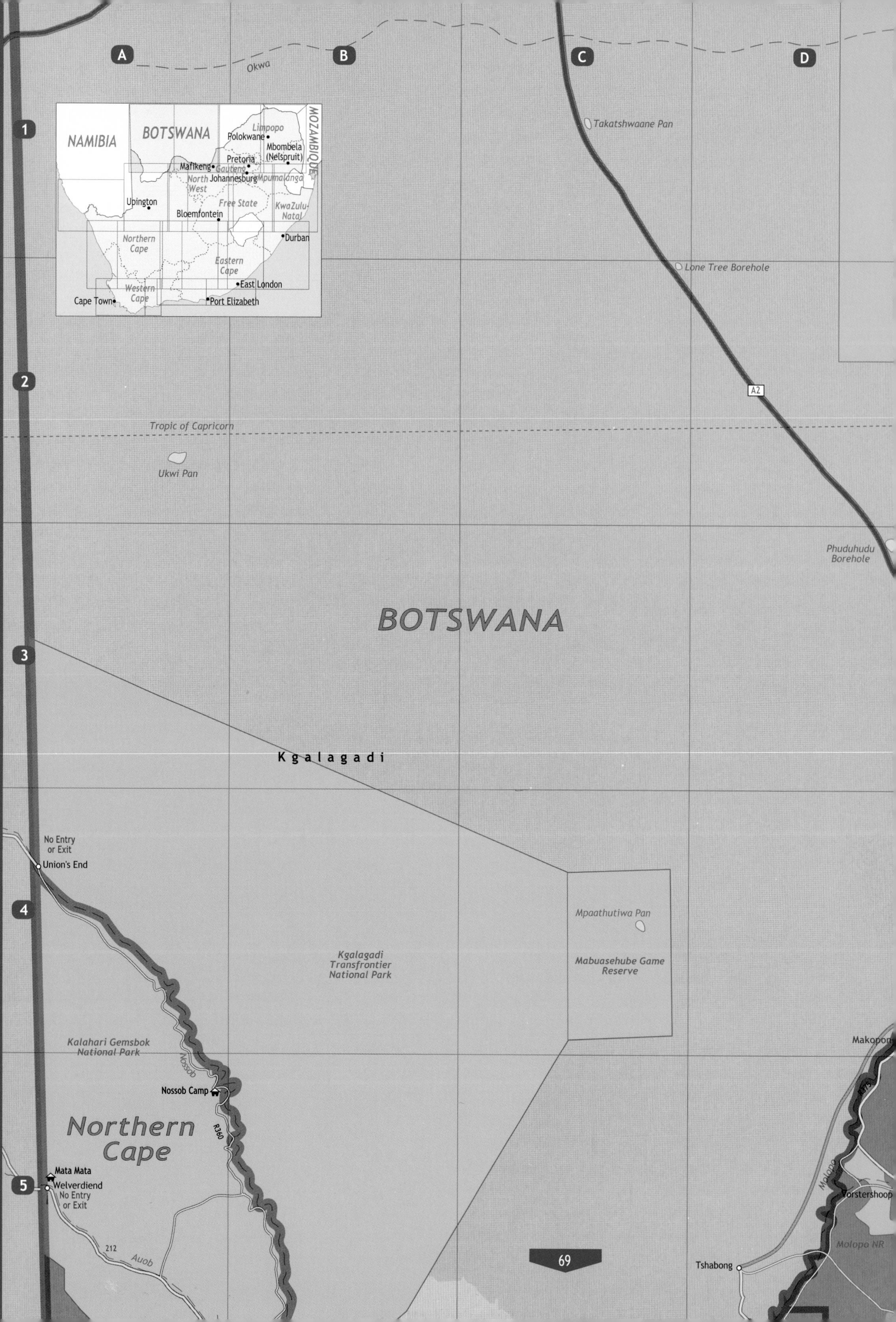

A B C D

1

2

Okwa

Takatshwaane Pan

Lone Tree Borehole

A2

Tropic of Capricorn

Ukwi Pan

Phuduhudu Borehole

BOTSWANA

3

Kgalagadi

No Entry or Exit

Union's End

4

Mpaathutiwa Pan

Mabuasehube Game Reserve

Kgalagadi Transfrontier National Park

Makopon

Kalahari Gemsbok National Park

Nossob

Nossob Camp

R360

Northern Cape

Mata Mata

5 Welverdiend No Entry or Exit

212

Auob

Molopo

orstershoop

69

Tshabong

Molopo NR

Inset map:

NAMIBIA BOTSWANA MOZAMBIQUE

Limpopo
Polokwane
Mbombela (Nelspruit)
Mafikeng Gauteng Pretoria
North West Johannesburg Mpumalanga
Upington Free State KwaZulu-Natal
Bloemfontein
Northern Cape
Durban
Eastern Cape
Western Cape East London
Cape Town Port Elizabeth

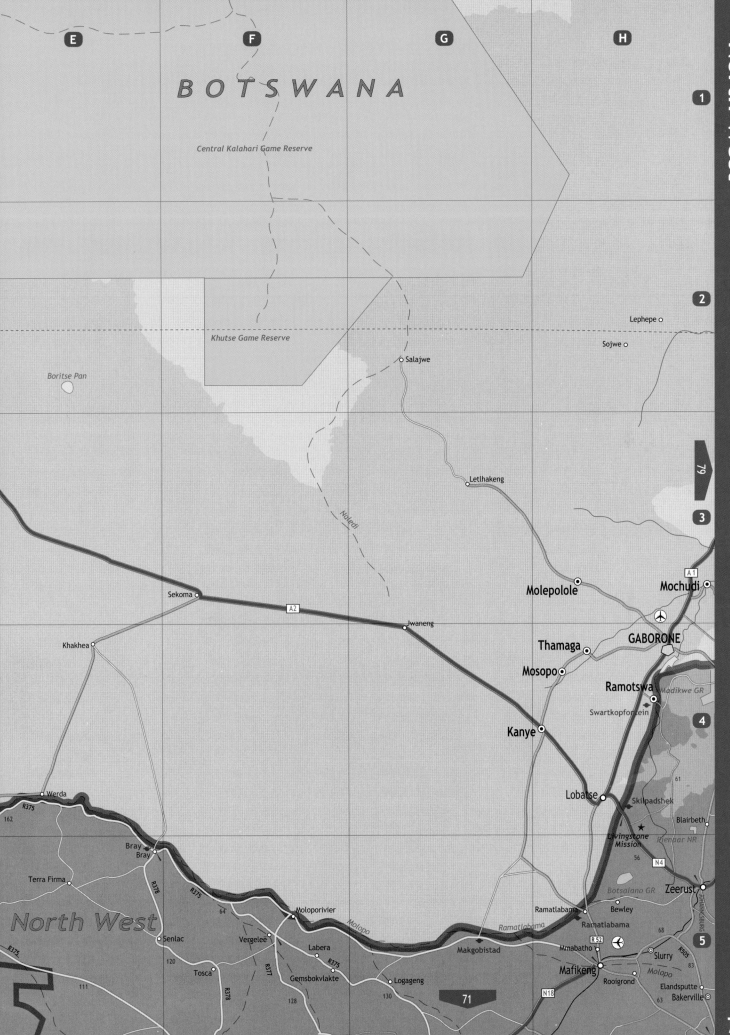

North West and Limpopo

*T*he North West province is a vast, hot, flattish region of bushveld and thorn, of lonely farmsteads, of fields of sunflowers, groundnuts, tobacco, and citrus, and of villages that sleep soundly in the sun. This is one of the great granaries of southern Africa, with endless fields of maize stretching out to the far horizon. Limpopo, which stretches up the lovely Waterberg and Soutpansberg ranges to the Limpopo River valley, is also largely farming country but more densely populated; its principal centre and capital is the pleasant town of Polokwane.

Route diagram (N1): Beit Bridge to Pretoria

km from Beit Bridge	Place	km from Pretoria
492 km	BEIT BRIDGE	0 km
476	Musina (16)	16
384	Louis Trichardt (Makhado) N1 (92)	108
267	POLOKWANE — Tzaneen R71 (95) (117)	225
210	Mokopane — Zebediela R518 (42) (57)	282
159	Mookgophong — Roedtan N11 (39) (51)	333
101	Bela-Bela (3) R516 (58)	391
0 km	PRETORIA N1 (101)	492 km

TRAVEL TIPS

All national roads in this area are tarred and generally in excellent condition; most of the secondary roads are gravelled and reasonably well maintained.

The stretch of road between Bela-Bela and Polokwane can get very busy over the Easter weekend. Holiday-makers travelling to the towns and game reserves of the Lowveld join a cavalcade of taxis and buses ferrying worshippers of the ZCC (Zion Christian Church) to their destination, Moria, near Polokwane. Traffic is congested and extreme caution is advised.

MAIN ATTRACTIONS

Sun City and Palace of the Lost City: luxury hotel-casino complex of pure innovation and fantasy.
Pilanesberg Game Reserve: great expanse of wildlife-rich habitat.
Bela-Bela: renowned for its curative springs; the Hydro Spa is of world standard.
Polokwane: principal town of Limpopo; nearby are the **Percy Fyfe Nature Reserve**, where several antelope species may be seen, and the interesting **Bakone Malapa Open-air Museum**, with traditional *kraal* and handicrafts.

Below: *The natural springs at Bela-Bela are not the only attraction at this world-class spa resort.*

A B C D

1

Serowe

Palapye

Northern Tuli Conservation Area
Reptile Footprints

Lotsane

Zanzibar
Platjan
Kopersuit   Usutu   Gregory
125   R572

B O T S W A N A

Mahalapye

Sherwood Ranch

Martin's Drift

Groblers Bridge
Tom Burke
Swartwater   Maasstroom   Tonash   De Gracht

Limpopo

2

R572   Beauty   Marnitz
75   N11
Baltimore   Woudkop   Steiloopbrug
Senwabarana

Makwate

Parr's Halt

Tropic of Capricorn

Stockpoort
R572   Monte Christo
R510
Oranjefontein
Ons Hoop

Mokolo
R518
Villa Nora
Janseput   Marken
160   178
Mogalakwena
Limburg   Matlala

Limpopo

77

Lephalale

R517   56   Afguns

Lapalala Wilderness GR

Gilead

Glen Alpine Dam

BLOUBERG

Blouberg NR

Mosomane   Spanwerk

Mokolo Dam
Mokala Dam NR
Elmeston   Hermanusdorings
R510   R517   41

Groesbeek
Mokamole
Tinmyne
R518
Mahwelereng   Mokopane
Moorddrif Monument

Percy Fyfe NR

3

Mochudi

Rooibokkraal   Rooibosbult
R510
66   Matlabas
Sentrum   Marakele NP   Vaalwater

Palala
Doorndraai Dam NR
Hanglipberge
Vanalphensvlei   Haakdoring
R520
Mineral Springs   82   R519   Mookgophong   Roedtan
R519   Crecy   75

N1
N11
81

Maricosdraai
Ben Alberts NR   2085 m   WATERBERGE
Rankin's
Alma   48
Klein-Sand   R517

Sikwane   Derdepoort
Kopfontein Gate
Kaya se Put
Madikwe GR

Thabazimbi
Dwaalboom
WITFONTEINRAND
1499 m
Middelwit   Koedoeskop   Leeuport
R511   R516   Mabula
Modimolle
R101   Middelfontein   104
Holme Park
R516   Nutfield
R33

Zwingli
Nietverdiend
R49   Silkaatskop   Gankuil
Moiatedi Dam
Bier   105   R510
Northam
R511

Rooiberg
Hot Mineral Springs
Bela-Bela   Settlers   R516   Tuinplaas
R576   54   Siyabuswa

4

81
Straatsdrif
Kromellenboog Dam
Marico Bosveld NR
Mabeskraal
Skuinsdrif   Mabaalstad
Rusverby
Zeerust   40   Groot-Marico   Swartruggens   88
N4

North West

Mogwase
Pilanesberg
1687 m
Pilanesberg Game Reserve
Sun City/Lost City
R565   R510
Millvale   121
Marikana
Paul Kruger's Cottage

Assen   Atlanta
Borakalalo Game Reserve
Moretele
Klipvoor Dam
Beestekraal
Rooikoppies Dam
Vaalkop Dam   125   Pansdrif
R556   R513

Radium   Pienaarsrivier
N1
Temba   Babelegi
Soutpan
Tswaing Crater and Museum
Hammanskraal
Mabopane
Ga-Rankuwa
Brits
38

Rust de Winter
Rust de Winter Nature Reserve
R573   Witnek   Dennilton

Mpumalanga
Kwamhlanga   Verena
Seringkop   R25
156

R544

5

Wondermere
Carlsonia   Mabaalstad   R509
Grootpan   Koster
131   Derby   R509

Bospoort Dam
48
Rustenburg
Syringa Tree Stump
R52   R24   MAGALIESBERG
Magaliesberg Nature Area
Skeerpoort
Gauteng
JOHANNESBURG
73

Kosmos   Hartbeespoort
Erasmia
N14
Centurion
N4

Swartwater
R513   PRETORIA
Rayton   R25
11
Cullinan
Vaalplaas
Bronkhorstspruit   Kromdraai
N4   116   Balmoral
eMalahleni (Witbank)

Limpopo and Mpumalanga

The eastern part of this region is dominated by the Great Escarpment, a spectacular compound of forest-mantled mountains, deep ravines, crystal-clear streams and delicate waterfalls. For sheer scenic beauty, few other parts of the country can compare with this imposing range, which rises near Mbombela (Nelspruit) and runs to the northeast for some 300km (186 miles). To the east of the escarpment lies the wildlife-rich Lowveld, where the vast Kruger National Park and a host of beautiful private reserves are situated.

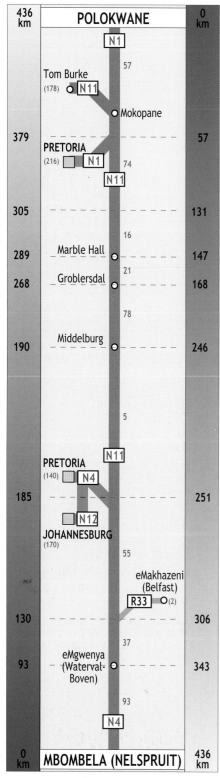

MAIN ATTRACTIONS

Pilgrim's Rest: a living showcase of the early gold-mining days.
Zebediela: South Africa's largest citrus estates are located here.
Polokwane: this is the principal town of Limpopo.
Tzaneen: little town surrounded by waterfalls and forests. Visit nearby **Magoebaskloof** and see the **Modjadjiskloof** realm of the **Modjadji Rain Queen** (source for Sir Rider Haggard's novel *She*) and the impressive cycad forest.
Loskop Dam Game Reserve: wildlife sanctuary around a large dam.
The Sunland Baobab: A 6000-year-old boabab tree near Modjadjiskloof; tel: 015 309 9039.

TRAVEL TIPS

Most of the roads are tarred, generally in excellent condition and well sign-posted. The climate is equable, though rainfall during the summer months, from November to February, often occurs in the form of sudden torrential down-pours which are accompanied by thunder and lightning. The storms tend to be brief, however, and there are very few days without long hours of sunshine.
A common feature of the escarpment is the occurrence of dense fog patches, and caution is therefore advised.
During the 19th and early 20th centuries malaria claimed the lives of many settlers in this area.
The disease is largely under control today, but travellers are strongly advised to take precautionary measures before entering the region.

Below: *The Blyde River winds its way through the magnificent canyon of the same name.*

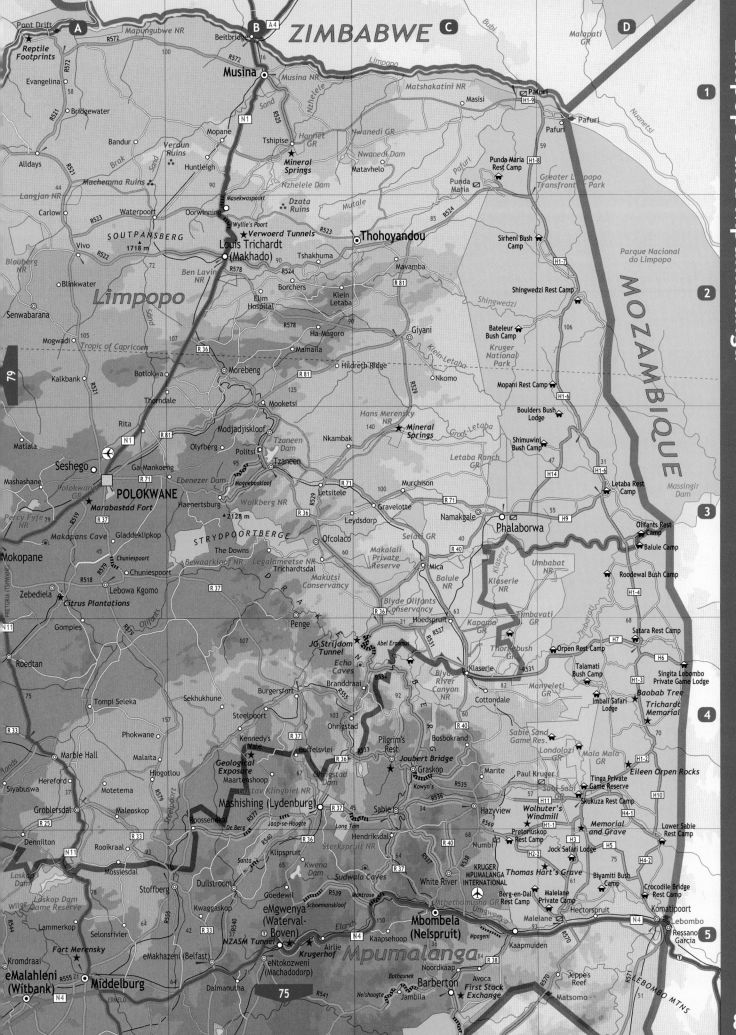

ZIMBABWE

MOZAMBIQUE

Limpopo

Kruger National Park

Mpumalanga

TOURIST AREA AND TEXT INDEX

Note: Numbers in **bold** denote photographs

83

86

Place	Grid	No.	Place	Grid	No.	Place	Grid	No.	Place	Grid	No.
Britstown	B2	64	Clanwilliam	D4	63	De Gracht	D1	79	Dwyka	G5	63
Broedersput	D2	71	Clarens	B4	73	De Hoek	D5	63	Dysselsdorp	A4	60
Bronkhorstspruit	C1	73	Clarkebury	C4	66	De Hoop	A4	60	East London	G4	61
Brooks Nek	D2	66	Clarkson	C5	60	De Klerk	B3	64	Eastpoort	E5	65
Bruintjieshoogte	E5	65	Clewer	C1	73	De Rust	A4	60	Edenburg	E1	65
Bucklands	B5	70	Clifford	B3	66	Dealesville	E4	71	Edendale	A1	67
Buffelsdrif	B5	60	Clocolan	A4	73	Deelfontein	C3	65	Edenville	B3	73
Buffelsvlei	B4	81	Coalville	C1	73	Deelpan	E1	71	Eendekuil	D5	63
Bulletrap	B1	62	Coega	E5	61	Delareyville	D2	71	Eksteenfontein	B5	68
Bultfontein	E4	71	Coerney	E4	61	Delmas	C1	73	Elands Height	C2	66
Bulwer	A1	67	Coffee Bay	D4	66	Delportshoop	C4	71	Elandsbaai	C4	62
Buntingville	D4	66	Cofimvaba	B4	66	Demistkraal	D5	60	Elandsdrift	E4	65
Burgersdorp	F3	65	Coghlan	C4	66	Deneysville	B2	73	Elandskraal	A4	75
Burgersfort	B4	81	Colchester	E5	61	Dennilton	A5	81	Elandslaagte	D4	73
Burgervilleweg	C2	65	Colenso	D4	73	Derby	B5	79	Elandsputte	E1	71
Butterworth	C4	66	Colesberg	D2	65	Derdepoort	A4	79	Elgin	B2	60
Cala	B3	66	Coleskeplaas	C5	60	Despatch	D5	60	Elim	C3	60
Cala Road	B3	66	Coligny	E1	71	Devon	C1	73	Elim Hospital	B2	81
Caledon	C3	60	Committees	F4	61	Devonlea	D2	71	Elliot	B3	66
Calitzdorp	E2	61	Commondale	B3	75	Dewetsdorp	F1	65	Elliotdale	C4	66
Calvert	B3	75	Concordia	C5	68	Dibeng	A3	70	Elmeston	C3	79
Calvinia	E3	63	Content	D4	71	Die Bos	E4	63	Eloff	C1	73
Cambria	C5	60	Conway	E4	65	Die Dam	C3	60	eMalahleni		
Cameron Glen	E4	65	Cookhouse	E5	65	Die Vlug	B5	60	(Witbank)	D1	73
Campbell	B4	70	Copperton	A1	64	Diemansputs	G1	63	eMakhazeni		
Candover	C3	75	Cornelia	C2	73	Dieput	C2	65	(Belfast)	B5	81
Cape St Francis	D5	60	Cottondale	C4	81	Dingleton	A3	70	eMangusi	D2	75
Cape Town	B2	60	Cradock	E4	65	Dirkiesdorp	A2	75	eMgwenya		
Carletonville	A1	73	Cramond	C2	69	Ditshipeng	B2	70	(Waterval-		
Carlisle Bridge	F5	65	Crecy	D4	79	Dlolwana	B4	75	Boven)	B5	81
Carlsonia	A5	79	Creighton	A2	67	Dohne	B5	66	eMkhondo (Piet		
Carlton	D3	65	Cullinan	D5	79	Donkerpoort	E2	65	Retief)	B2	75
Carnarvon	A3	64	Dabenoris	D5	68	Donnybrook	A2	67	eMpangeni	C5	75
Carolina	A1	75	Dagbreek	C4	69	Dordrecht	B3	66	eNtokozweni		
Cathcart	B4	66	Daggaboersnek	E5	65	Doringbaai	C4	62	(Machadodorp)	B5	81
Cedarville	D2	66	Daleside	B1	73	Doringbos	D4	63	eNtumeni	B5	75
Cederberg	D5	63	Dalmanutha	A1	75	Douglas	B5	70	Erasmia	B1	73
Centani	C5	66	Dalton	B1	67	Dover	B2	73	Ermelo	D2	73
Centurion	B1	73	Daniëlskuil	B3	70	Dovesdale	A1	73	eShowe	B5	75
Ceres	C1	60	Danielsrus	B3	73	Drennan	E4	65	Estcourt	D5	73
Chalumna	G4	61	Dannhauser	A3	75	Driefontein	D4	73	Evander	C2	73
Charl Cilliers	C2	73	Darling	B1	60	Droërivier	A4	64	Evangelina	A1	81
Charlestown	D3	73	Darnall	B5	75	Dullstroom	B5	81	Evaton	B2	73
Chieveley	D5	73	Daskop	A5	60	Dundee	A4	75	Excelsior	F5	71
Chintsa East	C5	66	Dasville	C2	73	Dupleston	F2	65	Fairfield	C3	60
Chrissiesmeer	A1	75	Davel	D2	73	Durban	B2	67	Faure	B2	60
Christiana	D3	71	Daveyton	C1	73	Durbanville	B2	60	Fauresmith	E1	65
Chuniespoort	A3	81	Dawn	G4	61	Dutywa	C4	66	Felixton	C5	75
Churchhaven	A1	60	De Aar	C2	65	Dwaal	D3	65	Ferreira	E5	71
Citrusdal	D5	63	De Brug	E5	71	Dwaalboom	A4	79	Ficksburg	B4	73
Clanville	B3	66	De Doorns	C1	60	Dwarskersbos	C5	62	Firgrove	B2	60

Name	Grid	Pg
Fish Hoek	B2	60
Flagstaff	D3	66
Florisbad	E4	71
Fochville	A2	73
Fort Beaufort	F5	65
Fort Brown	F5	65
Fort Donald	D3	66
Fort Hare	F4	61
Fort Mistake	D4	73
Fort Mtombeni	B5	75
Fouriesburg	B4	73
Frankfort	D3	73
Franklin	D2	66
Franschhoek	C2	60
Fransenhof	A1	64
Fraserburg	G4	63
Frere	D5	73
Ga-Mankoeng	B3	81
Gamoep	C1	62
Gansbaai	C3	60
Ganskuil	A4	79
Ganyesa	C1	71
Ga-Rankuwa	C5	79
Garies	B2	62
Garryowen	B3	66
Geluksburg	D4	73
Gelukspruit	B3	69
Gemsbokvlakte	F5	77
Gemvale	D3	66
Genadendal	C2	60
Geneva	F3	71
George	A5	60
Gerdau	E1	71
Germiston	B1	73
Geysdorp	D1	71
Giesenskraal	B2	64
Gilead	D3	79
Gingindlovu	B5	75
Giyani	C2	81
Gladdeklipkop	A3	81
Glencoe	A4	75
Glenconnor	D4	60
Glenmore Beach	A3	67
Glenrock	F5	71
Gloria	D1	73
Glückstadt	B4	75
Goedemoed	F2	65
Goedewil	B5	81
Golela	C3	75
Gompies	A4	81
Gonubie	G4	61
Goodhouse	C5	68
Gordon's Bay	B2	60
Gouda	B1	60
Gouritsmond	E3	61
Graaff-Reinet	D4	65
Graafwater	C4	62
Grabouw	B2	60
Grahamstown	F4	61
Granaatboskolk	E1	63
Graskop	C4	81
Grasmere	B1	73
Graspan	C5	71
Gravelotte	C3	81
Gregory	D1	79
Greylingstad	C2	73
Greystone	D4	60
Greyton	C2	60
Greytown	A5	75
Griquatown	A4	70
Groblersdal	A4	81
Groblershoop	D4	69
Groenriviers-mond	B3	62
Groenvlei	A3	75
Groesbeek	D3	79
Grondneus	B3	69
Groot-Brakrivier	A5	60
Grootdrif	D3	63
Grootdrink	C4	69
Groot Jongensfontein	E3	61
Grootkraal	A4	60
Groot-Marico	A5	79
Grootmis	A1	62
Grootpan	A5	79
Grootspruit	A3	75
Grootvlei	C2	73
Groutville	C1	67
Gumtree	A4	73
Haakdoring	D3	79
Haarlem	B5	60
Haenertsburg	B3	81
Haga-Haga	C5	66
Halcyon Drift	C3	66
Halfweg	E2	63
Ha-Magoro	B2	81
Hamburg	G4	61
Hammanskraal	C5	79
Hammarsdale	B1	67
Hankey	D5	60
Hanover	D3	65
Hanover Road	D3	65
Hantam	D3	63
Harding	A2	67
Harrisburg	F2	71
Harrisdale	B3	69
Harrismith	C4	73
Hartbeesfontein	F2	71
Hartbeespoort	C5	79
Hartebeeskop	B1	75
Hartswater	D3	71
Hattingspruit	A4	75
Hauptsrus	E2	71
Hawston	C3	60
Hazyview	C4	81
Hectorspruit	D5	81
Heerenlogement	C4	62
Heidelberg	B2	73
Heilbron	B2	73
Helpmekaar	A4	75
Helvetia	F1	65
Hendriksdal	C5	81
Hendrina	D1	73
Hennenman	F3	71
Herbertsdale	E2	61
Hereford	A4	81
Hermanus	C3	60
Hermanusdorings	C3	79
Herold	A5	60
Herolds Bay	A5	60
Herschel	B2	66
Hertzogville	D3	71
Het Kruis	D5	63
Heuningspruit	A3	73
Heydon	D3	65
Hibberdene	B2	67
Higg's Hope	A5	70
Highflats	A2	67
Hilandale	D1	60
Hildreth Ridge	B2	81
Hillandale	F5	63
Hilton	A1	67
Himeville	D1	66
Hlabisa	C4	75
Hlobane	B3	75
Hlogotlou	A4	81
Hluhluwe	C4	75
Hobeni	D4	66
Hobhouse	F5	71
Hoedspruit	C4	81
Hofmeyr	E3	65
Hogsback	A5	66
Holbank	A2	75
Holme Park	D4	79
Holmedene	C2	73
Hondefontein	G4	63
Hondeklipbaai	A2	62
Hoopstad	E3	71
Hopefield	B1	60
Hopetown	C1	65
Hotagterklip	C3	60
Hotazel	A2	70
Hottentotskloof	C1	60
Hout Bay	B2	60
Houtkraal	C2	65
Howick	A5	75
Humansdorp	D5	60
Huntleigh	B1	81
Hutchinson	B3	64
iMpendle	A1	67
Impisi	A3	67
iNanda	B1	67
Indwe	B3	66
Infanta	D3	60
Ingogo	D3	73
iNgwavuma	C3	75
iSipingo	B2	67
Iswepe	A2	75
Itsoseng	E1	71
iXopo	A2	67
Jacobsdal	C5	71
Jagersfontein	E1	65
Jaght Drift	F1	63
Jambila	C5	81
Jamestown	F3	65
Jammerdrif	A1	66
Jan Kempdorp	D3	71
Jansenville	D4	60
Janseput	C2	79
Jeffreys Bay	D5	60
Jeppe's Reef	D5	81
Joel's Drift	B4	73
Johannesburg	B1	73
Joubertina	C5	60
Jozini	C3	75
Kaapmuiden	C5	81
Kaapsehoop	C5	81
Kakamas	B4	69
Kalbaskraal	B2	60
Kalkbank	A2	81
Kalkwerf	C4	69
Kameel	D2	71
Kamiesberg	C2	62

Kamieskroon	B2	62	Klipplaat	C5	65	Kwaggaskop	B5	81	Logageng	G5	77
Kammiebos	C5	60	Kliprand	C2	62	KwaMashu	B1	67	Lohatlha	A3	70
Kanoneiland	C4	69	Klipspruit	B5	81	KwaMbonambi	C4	75	Long Hope	E5	65
Karatara	B5	60	Knapdaar	F2	65	Kwamhlanga	D5	79	Loskop	D5	73
Karee	E4	71	Knysna	B5	60	Kylemore	B2	60	Lothair	A1	75

Kareeboschkolk	E1	63	Koedoeskop	B4	79	Laaiplek	A1	60	Louis Trichardt		
Kareedouw	C5	60	Koegas	D5	69	Labera	F5	77	(Makhado)	B2	81
Karkams	B2	62	Koegrabie	C5	69	Ladismith	E1	61	Louisvale	C4	69
Karos	C4	69	Koffiefontein	D1	65	Lady Frere	B4	66	Louterwater	C5	60
Kasuka Road	F5	61	Koingnaas	A2	62	Lady Grey	B2	66	Louwsburg	B3	75
Katkop	E2	63	Kokstad	D2	66	Ladybrand	A5	73	Lower		
Kathu	A3	70	Komaggas	B1	62	Ladysmith	D4	73	Dikgatlhong	A2	70
Kaya se Put	A4	79	Komatipoort	D5	81	L'Agulhas	D3	60	Lower Pitseng	C2	66
Keate's Drift	A5	75	Komga	B5	66	Lahlangubo	C3	66	Loxton	A3	64
Kei Mouth	C5	66	Komkans	C3	62	Laingsburg	D1	60	Luckhoff	D1	65
Kei Road	B5	66	Kommandokraal	B5	64	Lambert's Bay	C4	62	Lundin's Nek	B2	66
Keimoes	B4	69	Kommetjie	B2	60	Lammerkop	A5	81	Luneberg	A3	75
Keiskammahoek	B5	66	Kommissiepoort	A5	73	Landplaas	C3	62	Lusikisiki	D3	66
Kempton Park	B1	73	Koopan Suid	B2	69	Langberg	E2	61	Luttig	A5	64
Kendal	C1	73	Koopmansfontein	C4	71	Langdon	C4	66	Lutzputs	B4	69
Kendrew	D5	65	Koosfontein	D2	71	Langebaan	A1	60	Lutzville	C4	62
Kenhardt	C5	69	Kootjieskolk	E3	63	Langholm	F4	61	Lykso	C2	71
Kenilworth	D4	71	Koperspruit	D1	79	Langklip	B4	69	Maartenshoop	B4	81
Kennedy's Vale	B4	81	Koppies	A2	73	Leandra	C1	73	Maasstroom	D1	79
Kenton on Sea	F5	61	Koringberg	B1	60	Lebowa Kgomo	A3	81	Mabaalstad	A5	79
Kestell	C4	73	Koringplaas	F5	63	Leeudoringstad	E2	71	Mabeskraal	A4	79
Kidd's Beach	G4	61	Kosmos	C5	79	Leeu-Gamka	G5	63	Mabopane	C5	79
Kimberley	C4	71	Koster	B5	79	Leeuport	C4	79	Mabula	C4	79
King William's			Kotzesrus	B3	62	Lehlohonolo	D2	66	Macleantown	B5	66
Town	B5	66	Koukraal	F2	65	Leipoldtville	C4	62	Maclear	C3	66
Kingsburgh	B2	67	Koup	E1	61	Lekfontein	F5	65	Madadeni	A3	75
Kingscote	D2	66	Koutjie	A5	60	Lekkersing	B5	68	Madibogo	D1	71
Kingsley	A3	75	Kraaifontein	B2	60	Lemoenshoek	D2	60	Madipelesa	C3	71
Kingswood	E3	71	Kraaldorings	E1	61	Lephalale	C2	79	Mafeteng	B1	66
Kinirapoort	C2	66	Kraankuil	C1	65	Letjiesbos	A5	64	Mafikeng	H5	77
Kinross	C1	73	Kransfontein	C4	73	Letsitele	B3	81	Mafube	D2	66
Kirkwood	D4	60	Kranskop	A5	75	Leydsdorp	B3	81	Magaliesburg	A1	73
Klaarstroom	A4	60	Kriel	C1	73	Libertas	B4	73	Magudu	C3	75
Klaserie	C4	81	Kromdraai	A5	81	Libode	D3	66	Mahlabatini	B4	75
Klawer	C4	62	Kroonstad	A3	73	Lichtenburg	E1	71	Mahlangasi	C3	75
Klein Drakenstein	B2	60	Krugers	E1	65	Lidgetton	A1	67	Mahwelereng	D3	79
Klein Letaba	B2	81	Krugersdorp	B1	73	Limburg	D3	79	Maizefield	D2	73
Klein Tswaing	C2	71	Kruidfontein	G5	63	Lime Acres	B4	70	Makwassie	E2	71
Kleinbegin	C4	69	Kruisfontein	D5	60	Lindeshof	C2	60	Malaita	A4	81
Kleinmond	B3	60	Kruisrivier	E1	61	Lindley	B3	73	Maleoskop	A4	81
Kleinpoort	D4	60	Kuboes	B4	68	Llandudno	B2	60	Malgas	D3	60
Kleinsee	A1	62	Kuilsriver	B2	60	Loch Vaal	B2	73	Malmesbury	B2	60
Klerksdorp	F2	71	Ku-Mayima	C3	66	Lochiel	B1	75	Mamaila	B2	81
Klerkskraal	A1	73	Kuruman	B3	70	Loerie	D5	60	Mamre	B2	60
Klipdale	C3	60	KwaDweshula	A2	67	Loeriesfontein	D3	63	Mandini	B5	75
Klipfontein	D1	73	KwaDukuza	C1	67	Lofter	E2	65	Mangeni	A4	75

Place	Grid	Pg	Place	Grid	Pg	Place	Grid	Pg	Place	Grid	Pg
Manthestad	D3	71	Middelburg	A5	81	Mount Fletcher	C2	66	Nieu-Bethesda	D4	65
Mantsonyane	C1	66	Middelburg	D3	65	Mount Frere	D3	66	Nieuwoudtville	D3	63
Mapumulo	B5	75	Middelfontein	D4	79	Mount Rupert	C3	71	Nigel	C1	73
Marakabei	C1	66	Middelpos	E4	63	Mount Stewart	D5	65	Nigramoep	B5	68
Marble Hall	A4	81	Middelwit	B4	79	Moyeni	B2	66	Nkambak	B3	81
Marburg	A3	67	Middleton	E5	65	Mpemvana	A3	75	Nkandla	B4	75
Marchand	B4	69	Midrand	B1	73	Mpethu	C5	66	Nkau	C2	66
Margate	A3	67	Migdol	D2	71	Mphaki	C2	66	Nkomo	C2	81
Maricosdraai	A3	79	Miller	C5	65	Mpolweni	A5	75	Nkwalini	B4	75
Marikana	B5	79	Millvale	B5	79	Mpumalanga	B1	67	Nobantu	D3	66
Marite	C4	81	Milnerton	B2	60	Mt Moorosi	C2	66	Nobhokhwe	B4	66
Marken	D2	79	Mirage	F2	71	Mthatha	D3	66	Noenieput	A3	69
Marnitz	C2	79	Misgund	B5	60	Mtkonjeneni	B4	75	Noll	B5	60
Marquard	A4	73	Mkambati	A3	67	Mtubatuba	C4	75	Nondweni	A4	75
Martin's Drift	C2	79	Mkuze	C3	75	Mtunzini	C5	75	Nongoma	B3	75
Marydale	D5	69	Mmabatho	H5	77	Mtwalume	B2	67	Noordhoek	B2	60
Mashashane	A3	81	Modderrivier	C5	71	Muden	A5	75	Noordkaap	C5	81
Mashishing (Lydenburg)	B4	81	Modimolle	C4	79	Muizenberg	B2	60	Noordkuil	C5	62
Masisi	C1	81	Modjadjiskloof	B3	81	Munster	A3	67	Normandien	D3	73
Matatiele	D2	66	Moeswal	D3	69	Munyu	C4	66	Northam	B4	79
Matavhelo	C1	81	Mogalakwena	D3	79	Murchison	C3	81	Norvalspont	E2	65
Matjiesfontein	D1	60	Mogwadi	A2	81	Murraysburg	C4	65	Nottingham Road	D5	73
Matjiesrivier	A4	60	Mogwase	B4	79	Musina	B1	81	Noupoort	D3	65
Matlabas	B3	79	Mohales Hoek	B2	66	Mynfontein	C3	65	Nqabarha	D4	66
Matlala	A3	81	Mokamole	D3	79	Nababeep	B1	62	Nqutu	A4	75
Matroosberg	C1	60	Mokopane	D3	79	Nabies	A4	69	Ntabamhlope	D5	73
Mavamba	C2	81	Moloporivier	F5	77	Nakop	A3	69	Ntabankulu	D3	66
Mazenod	B1	66	Molteno	F3	65	Namakgale	C3	81	Ntibane	C3	66
Mazeppa Bay	C5	66	Mont Pelaan	D3	73	Namies	D5	68	Ntseshe	C4	66
Mbashe Bridge	C4	66	Montagu	D2	60	Napier	C3	60	Ntshilini	D4	66
Mbazwana	D3	75	Monte Christo	C2	79	Nariep	B3	62	Ntywenka	C3	66
Mbombela (Nelspruit)	C5	81	Mooi River	D5	73	Nature's Valley	B5	60	Nutfield	D4	79
Mbotyi	A3	67	Mooifontein	E1	71	Ncanaha	E5	61	Nuwerus	C3	62
McGregor	C2	60	Mooketsi	B2	81	Ndumo	C2	75	Nuy	C2	60
Mdantsane	G4	61	Mookgophong	D4	79	Ndundulu	B4	75	Nyokana	C4	66
Meadows	A1	66	Moordkuil	C2	60	Ndwedwe	B1	67	Oatlands	C5	65
Melkbosstrand	B2	60	Moorreesburg	B1	60	Neilersdrif	C4	69	Obobogorap	A2	69
Melmoth	B4	75	Mopane	B1	81	Nelspoort	B4	64	Odendaalsrus	F3	71
Meltonwold	A3	64	Morebeng	B2	81	New Amalfi	D2	66	Ofcolaco	B3	81
Memel	D3	73	Morgan's Bay	C5	66	New England	B3	66	Ogies	C1	73
Merindol	F1	71	Morgenzon	D2	73	New Hanover	B1	67	Ohrigstad	B4	81
Merriman	C3	65	Morokweng	A2	70	New Machavie	F2	71	Okiep	B1	62
Merweville	G5	63	Morristown	B3	66	Newcastle	D3	73	Old Bunting	D4	66
Mesa	F1	71	Mortimer	E4	65	Ngcobo	C4	66	Old Morley	D4	66
Mesklip	B1	62	Moshesh's Ford	B3	66	Ngobeni	B3	75	Olifantshoek	A3	70
Meyerton	B2	73	Mosita	D1	71	Ngome	B3	75	Olyfberg	B3	81
Meyerville	C2	73	Mossel Bay	A5	60	Ngqamakhwe	C4	66	Omdraaisvlei	B2	64
Mgwali	B5	66	Mossiesdal	A5	81	Ngqeleni	D4	66	Onderstedorings	F2	63
Mica	C3	81	Motetema	A4	81	Ngqungqu	C4	66	Ons Hoop	C2	79
			Mothibistad	B2	70	Niekerkshoop	A5	70	Ontmoeting	C2	69
			Mount Ayliff	D3	66	Nietverdiend	A4	79	Oorwinning	B2	81

Place	Grid	Pg	Place	Grid	Pg	Place	Grid	Pg	Place	Grid	Pg
Oostermoed	B4	79	Philippolis Road	E2	65	Putsonderwater	D5	69	Riverside	A2	67
Orania	D1	65	Philipstown	D2	65	Qacha's Nek	D2	66	Riviersonderend	C2	60
Oranjefontein	C2	79	Phokwane	A4	81	Qamata	B4	66	Roamer's Rest	C2	66
Oranjerivier	C5	71	Phuthaditjhaba	C4	73	Qholhora Mouth	C5	66	Robert's Drift	C2	73
Oranjeville	B2	73	Pienaarsrivier	C4	79	Qhorha Mouth	C5	66	Robertson	C2	60
Orkney	F2	71	Piet Plessis	C1	71	Qiba	B3	66	Rode	D3	66
Osborn	B4	75	Pieter Meintjies	D1	60	Qoboqobo	C5	66	Rodenbeck	E5	71
oSizweni	A3	75	Pietermaritzburg	B1	67	Qoqodala	F4	65	Roedtan	A4	81
Ottosdal	E2	71	Piketberg	D5	63	Qudeni	A4	75	Roma	B1	66
Oudtshoorn	A4	60	Pilgrim's Rest	C4	81	Queensburgh	B2	67	Rondevlei	A5	60
Oukraal	C3	60	Pinetown	B1	67	Queenstown	F4	65	Roodebank	C2	73
Ouplaas	D3	60	Platbakkies	C2	62	Quko	C5	66	Roodepoort	B1	73
Oviston	E2	65	Plathuis	D2	60	Qumbu	D3	66	Rooiberg	C4	79
Owendale	B4	70	Platrand	D2	73	Radium	C4	79	Rooibokkraal	B3	79
Oyster Bay	D5	60	Plettenberg Bay	B5	60	Ramabanta	B1	66	Rooibosbult	B3	79
Paarl	B2	60	Plooysburg	C5	71	Ramatlabama	H5	77	Rooigrond	H5	77
Pacaltsdorp	A5	60	Pniel	B2	60	Ramsgate	A3	67	Rooikraal	A5	81
Paddock	A3	67	Pofadder	A5	69	Randalhurst	B4	75	Rooipan	C5	71
Pafuri	D1	81	Politsi	B3	81	Randburg	B1	73	Rooiwal	A2	73
Palala	D3	79	Polokwane	A3	81	Randfontein	B1	73	Roosboom	D4	73
Paleisheuwel	D5	63	Pomeroy	A4	75	Ratelfontein	C4	62	Roossenekal	B4	81
Palmerton	D3	66	Pongola	C3	75	Rawsonville	C2	60	Rorke's Drift	A4	75
Palmietfontein	B2	66	Pools	D5	63	Rayton	D5	79	Rosebank	A2	67
Pampierstad	C3	71	Port Alfred	F5	61	Redcliffe	D5	73	Rosedene	A4	64
Pampoenpoort	A3	64	Port Beaufort	D3	60	Reddersburg	F1	65	Rosendal	B4	73
Panbult	A2	75	Port Edward	A3	67	Redelinghuys	C5	62	Rosetta	D5	73
Pansdrif	C5	79	Port Elizabeth	E5	61	Redoubt	A3	67	Rosmead	D3	65
Papendorp	C4	62	Port Grosvenor	A3	67	Reebokrand	D1	65	Rossouw	B3	66
Papiesvlei	C3	60	Port Nolloth	B5	68	Reitz	B3	73	Rostrataville	E2	71
Papkuil	B4	70	Port Shepstone	B3	67	Reitzburg	A2	73	Rouxpos	E1	61
Park Rynie	B2	67	Port St Johns	D4	66	Reivilo	C3	71	Rouxville	A2	66
Parow	B2	60	Porterville	D5	63	Renosterkop	B4	64	Ruitersbos	E2	61
Parys	A2	73	Post Chalmers	E4	65	Renosterspruit	F2	71	Rust	B1	60
Patensie	D5	60	Postmasburg	A4	70	Restvale	B4	64	Rust de Winter	D4	79
Paternoster	B5	62	Potchefstroom			Rhodes	C2	66	Rustenburg	B5	79
Paterson	E4	61	(Tlokwe)	A2	73	Richards Bay	C5	75	Rustig	F3	71
Paul Roux	B4	73	Potfontein	C2	65	Richmond	C3	65	Rusverby	A5	79
Paulpietersburg	B3	75	Potsdam	G4	61	Riebeeckstad	F3	71	Saaifontein	G4	63
Pearly Beach	C3	60	Poupan	C1	65	Riebeek Kasteel	B1	60	Sabie	C4	81
Pearston	D5	65	Pretoria	C5	79	Riebeek East	E4	61	Sada	F4	65
Peddie	F4	61	Prieska	A5	70	Riebeek-Wes	B1	60	Sakrivier	E3	63
Pella	D5	68	Prince Albert	E1	61	Rietbron	B5	64	Saldanha	A1	60
Penge	B3	81	Prince Albert			Rietfontein	A2	69	Salem	F4	61
Perdekop	D2	73	Road	G5	63	Rietkuil	C3	73	Salpeterpan	C2	71
Petersburg	D4	65	Prince Alfred			Rietpoel	C3	60	Salt Lake	C5	71
Petrus Steyn	B3	73	Hamlet	C1	60	Rietpoort	B3	62	Salt Rock	C1	67
Petrusburg	D5	71	Pringle Bay	B3	60	Rietvlei	A5	75	Sand River Valley	D4	73
Petrusville	D1	65	Priors	E2	65	Rita	A3	81	Sandberg	C4	62
Phalaborwa	C3	81	Protem	D3	60	Ritchie	C5	71	Sandton	B1	73
Philadelphia	B2	60	Pudimoe	C3	71	River View	C4	75	Sandvlakte	C5	60
Philippolis	E2	65	Puntjie	E3	61	Riversdale	E2	61	Sannaspos	F5	71

Place	Grid	No.	Place	Grid	No.	Place	Grid	No.	Place	Grid	No.
Sannieshof	E1	71	Slurry	H5	77	Stoffberg	B5	81	The Heads	B5	60
Sasolburg	B2	73	Smithfield	A2	66	Stofvlei	C2	62	The Ranch	A5	75
Sauer	C5	62	Smitskraal	C5	60	Stompneusbaai	B5	62	Theron	F4	71
Scarborough	B2	60	Sneeukraal	A4	64	Stoneyridge	D3	66	Theunissen	F4	71
Scheepersnek	A3	75	Sodium	B2	64	Stormberg	F3	65	Thohoyandou	C2	81
Schmidtsdrif	C4	71	Soebatsfontein	B2	62	Stormsrivier	C5	60	Thorndale	A2	81
Schoombee	E3	65	Somerset East	E5	65	Stormsvlei	D2	60	Thornville	B1	67
Schweizer-Reneke	D2	71	Somerset West	B2	60	Straatsdrif	A4	79	Three Sisters	B4	64
Scottburgh	B2	67	Somkele	C4	75	Strand	B2	60	Tierfontein	E3	71
Sea Park	B3	67	Sonstraal	D2	69	Strandfontein	C4	62	Tierpoort	F1	65
Sea View	D5	60	Southbroom	A3	67	Struisbaai	D3	60	Tina Bridge	D3	66
Secunda	C2	73	Southeyville	B4	66	Strydenburg	C1	65	Tinmyne	D3	79
Sedgefield	B5	60	Southwell	F5	61	Strydpoort	E2	71	Tolwe	D2	79
Seekoegat	A5	64	Soutpan	C5	79	Studtis	C4	60	Tom Burke	C2	79
Sekhukhune	B4	81	Soweto	B1	73	Stutterheim	B5	66	Tombo	D4	66
Selonsrivier	A5	81	Spanwerk	B3	79	Summerstrand	E5	61	Tompi Seleka	A4	81
Sendelingsdrif	A4	68	Spes Bona	A2	73	Sun City/Lost City	B5	79	Tonash	D1	79
Senekal	A4	73	Spitskopvlei	D4	65	Sunland	E4	61	Tongaat	B1	67
Senlac	E5	77	Spoegrivier	B2	62	Sutherland	F4	63	Tontelbos	E3	63
Sentrum	B3	79	Spring Valley	F4	65	Sutton	A3	70	Tosca	F5	77
Senwabarana	A2	81	Springbok	B1	62	Suurbraak	D2	60	Touws River	C1	60
Seringkop	D5	79	Springfontein	E2	65	Swaershoek	E5	65	Trawal	C4	62
Seshego	A3	81	Springs	C1	73	Swartberg	D2	66	Trichardt	C2	73
Setlagole	D1	71	Spytfontein	C4	71	Swartkops	E5	61	Trichardtsdal	B3	81
Settlers	D4	79	St Faith's	A2	67	Swartmodder	B3	69	Triple Streams	C3	66
Sevenoaks	A5	75	St Francis Bay	D5	60	Swartplaas	A1	73	Trompsburg	E1	65
Severn	A2	70	St Helena Bay	C5	62	Swartputs	B4	70	Tsazo	C4	66
Seweweekspoort	E1	61	St Lucia	C4	75	Swartruggens	A5	79	Tshakhuma	B2	81
Seymour	F5	65	St Marks	B4	66	Swartwater	C1	79	Tshani	D4	66
Sezela	B2	67	Staansaam	B2	69	Swellendam	D2	60	Tshipise	B1	81
Shaka's Rock	C1	67	Stafford's Post	A2	67	Swempoort	B3	66	Tsineng	A2	70
Shakaskraal	C1	67	Standerton	C2	73	Swinburne	C4	73	Tsitsa Bridge	D3	66
Shannon	E5	71	Stanford	C3	60	Syfergat	A3	66	Tsoelike	D2	66
Sheepmoor	A2	75	Steekdorings	C2	71	Tafelberg	D3	65	Tsolo	D3	66
Sheldon	E5	65	Steelpoort	B4	81	Tainton	C5	66	Tsomo	B4	66
Sherborne	D3	65	Steilloopbrug	D2	79	Taleni	C4	66	Tugela Ferry	A4	75
Sidwadweni	D3	66	Steilrand	B3	75	Tarkastad	F4	65	Tugela Mouth	B5	75
Sigoga	D2	66	Steinkopf	C5	68	Taung	D3	71	Tuinplaas	D4	79
Silkaatskop	A4	79	Stella	D1	71	Temba	C5	79	Tulbagh	C1	60
Silutshana	A4	75	Stellenbosch	B2	60	Tembisa	B1	73	Tunnel	C1	60
Silver Streams	B4	70	Sterkaar	C3	65	Terra Firma	E5	77	Tweefontein	E4	63
Simon's Town	B3	60	Sterkspruit	B2	66	Teviot	E4	65	Tweeling	C3	73
Sinksabrug	A5	60	Sterkstroom	F3	65	Teza	C4	75	Tweespruit	F5	71
Sir Lowry's Pass	B2	60	Sterling	G3	63	Thaba Chitja	C2	66	Tyira	D3	66
Sishen	A3	70	Steynsburg	E3	65	Thaba 'Nchu	F5	71	Tylden	B4	66
Sittingbourne	B5	66	Steynsrus	A3	73	Thaba Tseka	C1	66	Tzaneen	B3	81
Siyabuswa	A4	81	Steytlerville	C4	60	Thabazimbi	B4	79	Ubombo	C3	75
Skeerpoort	C5	79	Stilfontein	F2	71	The Crags	B5	60	Ugie	C3	66
Skipskop	D3	60	Still Bay East	E3	61	The Downs	B3	81	Uitenhage	D5	60
Skuinsdrif	A5	79	Still Bay West	E3	61	The Haven	D4	66	Uitkyk	C1	62
			Stockpoort	B2	79				Uitspankraal	D4	63